LEARN GERMAN IN 100 DAYS

THE 100% NATURAL METHOD TO FINALLY GET RESULTS WITH GERMAN!

BEGINNER

NATURA LINGUA

LEARN GERMAN IN 100 DAYS

TABLE OF CONTENTS

WELCOME

Imagine: you're walking around in Berlin, understanding and speaking German naturally. Phrases spontaneously emerge in your mind, and you navigate this new language with ease and fluidity.

That's the goal of this manual.

If you're reading these lines, it's because you wish to master German. Whether for work or pleasure, the goal remains the same: to achieve it. The problem lies in the lack of time. Good courses to learn German in English are rare, and often, the available methods are complicated or ineffective.

But your motivation is intact! That's why you've tried apps promising wonders in just a few minutes a day. The result? More time spent collecting badges than acquiring real skills in German. You've tried traditional textbooks, often too complex and focused on grammar. Perhaps you've even considered classical courses, incompatible with your schedule.

My name is François, and I'm French. I am well acquainted with this situation.

A few years ago, I went to do a year of volunteering in Ukraine. To be effective, I had to quickly learn Ukrainian, Russian and English. But most learning resources were either too superficial or too complex.

Even worse, despite my motivation and long hours in front of my screen or immersed in manuals, the results were not forthcoming. I felt frustrated, angry, wondering why language learning seemed so easy for some and so difficult for me.

I was about to give up, thinking I was not cut out for languages.

Then, one evening, I met an English polyglot who spoke 11 languages. Impressed by his linguistic abilities, I asked him for his secret. His answer, as simple as it was unexpected, was that one should not study a language, but live it! One must learn a new language as one learned their mother tongue.

Intrigued, I followed his advice.

After all, I hadn't learned my mother tongue through conjugation tables or collecting badges. No, I learned French by imitating those around me, by communicating with my friends and family.

So, I abandoned my textbooks and removed the conjugation tables from the walls of my room.

I started listening to podcasts in English, watching movies in Ukrainian and Russian, and engaging in my first conversations. Forgetting grammar and conjugation, I simply used these languages. The results were quick to come: I increasingly understood daily conversations, with words and phrases naturally coming to mind.

My English friend was right: it worked.

Just as it's more effective to learn to swim by jumping into the water rather than reading a book on swimming, learning a foreign language is done by immersing oneself in the language, practicing conversation, listening, and adapting to the culture and linguistic nuances, rather than limiting oneself to the theoretical study of grammar rules and vocabulary.

This is the approach I propose in this Natura Lingua manual.

From the first lesson, you will fully immerse yourself in German.

In a few days, or even weeks, you will start to build a lexical foundation and mental mechanisms that will allow you to understand and communicate naturally in most daily situations.

Be aware, Natura Lingua is not a miracle solution. To get results, you will need to follow one lesson a day for 100 days.

But if you're ready to make this effort, then anyone can succeed with our method, based directly on the mechanisms that allowed you to learn your mother tongue.

If you've already learned your mother tongue, why couldn't you learn German?

Viel Erfolg,

François

THE NATURALINGUA METHOD

Natura Lingua offers you a natural and intuitive approach that transforms the language learning experience. Every educational content is meticulously optimized to enable you to acquire a new language up to 10 times faster and more efficiently than traditional methods.

Each Natura Lingua manual is based on four innovative principles that reinvent the way languages are learned.

1. The Funnel Principle

We've rigorously analyzed and filtered hundreds of thousands of words to retain only those that are essential in daily conversations. Thanks to this principle, you quickly develop a high level of understanding without wasting your time on superfluous terms.

2. Contextual Assimilation

Each term is introduced in a natural setting, reflecting common daily interactions. The result? A smooth assimilation of hundreds of terms and expressions, without ever feeling like you're actually studying.

3. Progressive Overload

Each lesson meticulously presents new words while reintroducing those already studied. Thus, day by day, you continuously progress while consolidating what you've learned.

4. Multiple Integrated Revisions

Gone are the days when vocabulary seemed to evaporate from your memory. Our unique method ensures that each term is reintroduced at strategic intervals in subsequent lessons. You revisit each term up to four times, reinforcing its memorization without even realizing it.

The Mechanism

What makes "Natura Lingua" so effective is its natural and gradual learning. Each lesson introduces new words in bold while reusing words from previous lessons. Additionally, each lesson is enriched with a "Grammatical Note" to illuminate key aspects of the language and a "Cultural Note" to avoid faux pas during conversations with natives.

Is It For Me?

If you're looking to speak a new language without getting lost in the intricacies of grammar, this manual is for you. However, if you love complex grammatical rules and endless vocabulary lists, then this manual is not for you.

Integrating the Manual Into Your Daily Life

Create a routine: dedicate a slot each day for your 15-minute lesson. A coffee in hand, your manual open in front of you, and off you go!

NB. I highly recommend downloading the audio that accompanies the lessons. It will greatly enhance your understanding and pronunciation. Using this manual without the audio is like enjoying toast without jam: you're missing the essence.

ADDITIONAL RESOURCES

DOWNLOAD THE RESOURCES ASSOCIATED WITH THIS MANUAL AND GREATLY ENHANCE YOUR CHANCES OF SUCCESS.

Scan this QR code to access them:

SCAN ME

☞ **https://www.natura-lingua.com/download**

• **Optimize your learning with audio:** To significantly improve your language skills, we strongly advise you to download the audio files accompanying this manual. This will enhance your listening comprehension and pronunciation.

• **Enhance your learning with flashcards:** Flashcards are excellent tools for vocabulary memorization. We highly encourage you to use them to maximize your results. Download our set of cards, specially designed for this manual.

• **Join our learning community:** If you're looking to connect with other language enthusiasts through "Natura Lingua", we invite you to join our online group. In this community, you'll have the opportunity to ask questions, find learning partners, and share your progress.

• **Explore more with other Natura Lingua manuals:** If you like this method, note that there are other similar manuals for different languages. Discover our complete collection of manuals to enrich your linguistic learning experience in a natural and progressive way.

We are here to support you in learning the target language. For optimal results, we highly recommend downloading the audio and using the flashcards. These additional resources are designed to further facilitate your journey.

Happy learning!

BEFORE BEGINNING

DEBUNKING MYTHS ABOUT LEARNING GERMAN

German, with its reputation for lengthy compound words and the dauntingly complex case system, often intimidates potential learners before they even begin. However, many of the preconceived notions about learning German are based on myths rather than reality. These misconceptions can deter people from embracing a language that opens doors to rich cultural experiences and opportunities. Let's debunk five common myths and shed light on the true nature of learning German.

Myth 1: German is Exceptionally Hard to Learn

One of the most pervasive myths is that German is an exceptionally hard language to learn, especially for English speakers. This belief is misleading. English and German share the same Germanic root, making many aspects of the language surprisingly familiar. Vocabulary, sentence structure, and even some grammar rules have similarities. While German has its complexities, like any language, learners

3

often find that the initial learning curve isn't as steep as they feared.

Myth 2: You Need to Master the Grammar to Speak German

Another common misconception is that flawless grammar is a prerequisite for speaking German. While grammar is important, perfection is not a requirement for effective communication. Many learners find that focusing on conversational skills and practical vocabulary allows them to engage in meaningful conversations long before they've mastered every grammatical rule. Success stories abound of people who've traveled or worked in German-speaking countries with a basic grasp of the language, improving significantly through immersion and practice.

Myth 3: German Pronunciation is Impossible to Master

German pronunciation may seem daunting at first, with its guttural sounds and the infamous "ch" sound. However, pronunciation is a skill that improves with practice. Many learners find that with consistent listening and speaking practice, German pronunciation becomes much more manageable. The key is exposure and repetition, not inherent linguistic talent.

Myth 4: It Takes Years to Become Fluent

The timeline to fluency is a common concern, with many believing it takes years to achieve any level of comfort in

German. While becoming fluent does require time and dedication, progress can be made much faster than many anticipate. Setting realistic goals, consistent practice, and immersion (even if it's through media or online conversations) can accelerate the learning process. Many learners achieve conversational fluency within months, not years.

Myth 5: You Can't Learn German as an Adult

The belief that language learning is only for children is not only false but also discouraging. Adults are capable of learning new languages, including German, with great success. While children may have advantages in pronunciation and learning through immersion, adults often have stronger motivation, better study habits, and a deeper understanding of grammatical concepts. Success stories of adults achieving fluency in German later in life are a testament to this.

The real challenge of learning German isn't wrapped up in its grammatical cases or vocabulary size but in persistence and consistency. The journey to learning any language is a marathon, not a sprint. It requires regular practice, exposure, and a willingness to make mistakes and learn from them.

Learning German, like any language, comes with its set of challenges. However, the myths surrounding its difficulty often exaggerate these challenges, deterring potential learners. By debunking these myths, we can approach German with a more positive and realistic perspective. The journey to fluency is personal and varied, filled with its own successes and setbacks. The key is to persist, stay motivated, and enjoy the rich experiences that come with learning a new language. The real challenge isn't in the language itself but in the commitment to keep learning and growing.

WHY LEARNING GERMAN?

If you're reading this text, it's because you're interested in learning German. That's a fantastic choice! German is not just a language; it's a key to a rich cultural heritage and a multitude of opportunities. Let's talk about motivation. It's the fuel that keeps the engine of learning running, even when the road gets tough. Here are seven sources of inspiration to stimulate your desire to learn German, each designed to ignite your passion and keep your spirits high on this linguistic journey.

1. **Unlock the Door to Culture:** German is the language of Goethe, Kafka, and Beethoven. Learning German opens up the treasure chest of German literature, music, art, and philosophy. Imagine reading Faust in its original language or understanding the lyrics of a hauntingly beautiful Schubert Lied. The cultural richness of the German-speaking world is an endless source of inspiration.

. . .

2. **Career Opportunities:** Germany is Europe's largest economy and home to numerous international corporations. Knowing German can significantly boost your career prospects, not just in Germany, Austria, and Switzerland, but in many other parts of the world where German companies have a strong presence. It's a language that can open doors to exciting job opportunities.

3. **Travel and Exploration:** Speaking German makes traveling in German-speaking countries a much richer experience. You can interact with locals, understand the culture more deeply, and navigate your way through cities and countryside with ease. Every conversation, every sign, and every menu becomes an opportunity to learn and grow.

4. **Educational Advantages:** Germany offers a wealth of educational opportunities, including many programs taught in English. However, knowing German can provide access to a broader array of scholarships, programs, and resources. It's a smart choice for anyone considering studying abroad.

5. **Brain Health:** Learning a new language is a fantastic workout for your brain. It improves memory, enhances problem-solving skills, and even delays the onset of dementia. German, with its logical structure and clear rules, is particularly good for developing cognitive abilities.

.   .   .

6. **Personal Satisfaction:** There's a profound sense of achievement in being able to communicate in a new language. Each new word, sentence, and conversation in German is a step towards becoming a more global citizen. It's a personal challenge with very rewarding outcomes.

7. **Connect with Others:** German is spoken by over 100 million people worldwide. Learning German can help you make new friends, connect with family members, or even find love. Language is all about connection, and German is your ticket to a whole new community.

In conclusion, let this be your call to action: Embrace the challenge of learning German with open arms and an open heart. Remember, every journey begins with a single step, and every language learner was once a beginner. Don't let fear of mistakes or the difficulty of the language deter you. The rewards of speaking German far outweigh the challenges. Keep pushing forward, keep practicing, and soon, you'll find yourself conversing with ease. Your German adventure awaits, and it's going to be an incredible ride. Viel Erfolg! (Good luck!)

THE POLYGLOTS' SECRET

The gift of speaking multiple languages is often seen as a rare talent, reserved for a few exceptional individuals. However, the journeys of Giuseppe Mezzofanti and Kato Lomb, two renowned polyglots, demonstrate that this ability can be accessible to all with the right approach and unwavering determination.

Giuseppe Mezzofanti, a native of Bologna, made history with his incredible ability to learn languages. From his childhood, he showed an extraordinary capacity to absorb and master languages. One story tells how he learned Albanian in just a few days to communicate with a group of refugees. This talent for languages allowed him to become a valuable cultural and religious intermediary, aiding understanding between various nationalities and beliefs. His method, centered on immersion and interaction, paved the way for a more dynamic and engaged approach to language learning.

Kato Lomb, a self-taught Hungarian linguist, defied conventions by learning over 16 languages without formal training. Her passion for reading led her to explore languages through books, immersing herself in novels and texts in their original language. She often shared how each new language learned opened a window to a new culture, enriching her understanding of the world. Her pragmatic approach and love for continual learning proved that the language barrier is not insurmountable.

Learning multiple languages is often seen as an insurmountable mountain, but Mezzofanti and Lomb show that this perception is misleading. Success in polyglotism is not based on innate talent but on an effective method and regular practice. Their example highlights the importance of immersing oneself in the language through reading, listening, and especially, conversing with native speakers.

Language learning opens many doors, both professionally and personally. It enables a better understanding of cultures, fosters empathy and tolerance, and offers diverse career opportunities. Mezzofanti and Lomb both used their linguistic skills to facilitate communication between cultures and enrich their own understanding of the world.

Begin your language learning journey with curiosity and an open mind. Each new language learned is an adventure in itself, an exploration of a new culture and a new way of thinking. Don't be afraid to make mistakes, as they are essential to learning. Remember, the path to polyglotism is gradual and rewarding. As Kato Lomb said, "Language is the only thing worth knowing even poorly."

The journeys of Mezzofanti and Kato Lomb demonstrate that polyglotism is not an inaccessible mystery, but a tangible reality for those who choose to engage with it. Their legacy encourages us to embrace linguistic and cultural diversity, reminding us that, in the quest for language learning, the journey is as important as the destination.

INSTRUCTIONS

SIMPLE GERMAN PRONUNCIATION GUIDE FOR ENGLISH SPEAKERS

Welcome to your quick guide to German pronunciation! This guide will help you get started with the basics. Remember, practice makes perfect, so try to listen to native speakers and repeat after them whenever you can.

Vowels

- **A** sounds like the 'a' in "father." Example: Mann (man)
- **E** can sound like the 'e' in "met" or the 'a' in "fate." Context will guide you. Example: Bett (bed), See (lake)
- **I** sounds like the 'ee' in "see." Example: Kind (child)
- **O** sounds like the 'o' in "so." Example: Sonne (sun)
- **U** sounds like the 'oo' in "food." Example: Hund (dog)
- **Ä** sounds somewhat like the 'a' in "cat." Example: Bär (bear)

- **Ö** has no direct English equivalent but try shaping your mouth as if to say 'e' (as in "bed") and then say 'o' (as in "so"). Example: schön (beautiful)
- **Ü** also has no direct English equivalent. Shape your mouth to say 'ee' (as in "see") and then try to say 'oo' (as in "food"). Example: über (over)

Consonants

- **B, D, F, K, L, M, N, P, T** are pronounced similarly to English.
- **G** at the beginning of words is like the 'g' in "go." At the end of a word, it's softer, more like the 'g' in "singe."
- **H** is pronounced as in English when it starts a word. When it follows a vowel, it often makes the vowel long and is itself silent.
- **J** is pronounced like the 'y' in "yes." Example: ja (yes)
- **R** is more guttural than in English. Think of a soft gargle in the back of your throat.
- **S** at the beginning of words or syllables is like the 'z' in "zebra." Between vowels, it's like the 's' in "see."
- **V** is pronounced like the 'f' in "fish." Example: Vater (father)
- **W** is pronounced like the 'v' in "vase." Example: Wasser (water)
- **Z** is pronounced like "ts" in "cats." Example: Zeit (time)

Special Consonant Combinations

- **CH** has two sounds. After "a," "o," "u," and "au," it's like a soft, throaty "h" with no English equivalent (try to say "hue" with the back of your throat). After "e," "i," "ä," "ö," "ü," it's softer, like the 'h' in "hue."
- **SCH** is like the 'sh' in "shoe." Example: Schule (school)
- **SP** and **ST** at the beginning of words sound like "shp" and "sht," respectively. Example: Stadt (city)

Final Tips

- **Stress** is usually on the first syllable in German words.
- **Long and Short Vowels:** Pay attention to vowel length; it can change the meaning of a word. Double consonants after a vowel usually indicate that the vowel is short.

Practice these sounds, and don't be afraid to exaggerate them as you learn. Listening to native speakers and repeating after them is one of the best ways to improve your pronunciation. Viel Erfolg! (Good luck!)

HOW TO USE THIS MANUAL

Phase No. 1:

1. Read the text in the language you are learning out loud, while listening to the corresponding audio (to be downloaded).
2. Try to translate the text into English, without consulting the translation.
3. Check with the official translation to complete yours.

This phase facilitates the assimilation of the language structure and vocabulary and reinforces understanding.

1. **Привіт**, як справи?
2. Добре, **дякую**. А у вас?
3. Теж добре, дякую. Доброго ранку!
4. **Доброго ранку!** Чи можу я вам допомогти?
5. **Будь ласка**, де тут банк?
6. Прямо за рогом. До зустрічі!
7. **Дякую!** До побачення!
8. **Доброго дня!**
9. **Добрий вечір! Доброї ночі!**

✤ In Ukrainian, nouns change their endings based on whether they are masculine, feminine, or neuter.

1. **Hello**, how are you?
2. Good, **thank you** And you?
3. Also good, **thank you. Good morning!**
4. **Good morning!** Can I help you with anything?
5. **Please**, where is the bank here?
6. Just around the corner. **See you!**
7. **Thank you! Goodbye!**
8. **Good day!**
9. **Good evening! Good night!**

✤ In Ukraine, it's traditional to greet close friends with three kisses on the cheeks.

Hello, how are you doing?
Doing well, thank you. And you?
Also doing well, thank you. Good morning
Good morning! Can I assist you with something?
Yes, please. Where is the bank located?
It's just around the corner. See you later!
Thank you! Goodbye!
Have a good day!
Good evening! Good night!

Phase No. 1

Phase No. 2 (starting from lesson No. 7):

1. For each lesson starting from No. 7, first translate the text of that lesson (No. 7, No. 8, etc.) from the target language into English.
2. Then, go back 6 lessons and translate the English version of that lesson's text from English back into the target language, without referring to the original text.
3. Compare your translation with the original text of that lesson and adjust if necessary.
4. Read aloud the original text of that lesson, while listening to the audio.

This phase stimulates the activation of already acquired vocabulary and promotes the improvement of your communication skills.

1. Привіт, як справи?
2. Добре, дякую. А у вас?
3. Теж добре, дякую. Доброго ранку!
4. Доброго ранку! Чи можу я вам допомогти?
5. Будь ласка, де тут банк?
6. Прямо за рогом. До зустрічі!
7. Дякую! До побачення!
8. Доброго дня!
9. Добрий вечір! Доброї ночі!

✦ In Ukrainian, nouns change their endings based on whether they are masculine, feminine, or neuter.

Hello, how are you doing?
Doing well, thank you. And you?
Also doing well, thank you. Good morning!
Good morning! Can I assist you with something?
Yes, please. Where is the bank located?
It's just around the corner. See you later!
Thank you! Goodbye!
Have a good day!
Good evening! Good night!

26

1. **Hello,** how are you?
2. Good, **thank you.** And you?
3. Also good, **thank you. Good morning!**
4. **Good morning!** Can I help you with anything?
5. **Please,** where is the bank here?
6. Just around the corner. **See you!**
7. **Thank you!** Goodbye!
8. **Good day!**
9. **Good evening! Good night!**

✦ In Ukraine, it is common to greet close friends with three kisses on the cheeks.

Привіт, як справи?
Добре, дякую. А у вас?
Теж добре, дякую. Доброго ранку!
Доброго ранку! Чи можу я вам
допомогти?
Будь ласка, де тут банк?
Прямо за рогом. До зустрічі!
Дякую! До побачення!
Доброго дня!
Добрии вечір! Доброї ночі!

27

Phase No. 2

Continue in the same way for the following lessons. For example, for lesson No. 8, first translate the text of lesson No. 8 from the target language into English, then translate the text of lesson No. 2 from English back into the target language, and so on.

Additionally, every 10 lessons, a small challenge awaits you to put your knowledge into practice.

Note: Your translations do not need to match the manual texts perfectly, but they should convey a similar meaning. If you are using the paper version of the manual, note your translations directly at the bottom of the text, or else use a separate notebook.

ADDITIONAL RESOURCES

DOWNLOAD THE RESOURCES ASSOCIATED WITH THIS MANUAL AND GREATLY ENHANCE YOUR CHANCES OF SUCCESS.

Scan this QR code to access them:

SCAN ME

☞ **https://www.natura-lingua.com/download**

• **Optimize your learning with audio:** To significantly improve your language skills, we strongly advise you to download the audio files accompanying this manual. This will enhance your listening comprehension and pronunciation.

- **Enhance your learning with flashcards:** Flashcards are excellent tools for vocabulary memorization. We highly encourage you to use them to maximize your results. Download our set of cards, specially designed for this manual.

- **Join our learning community:** If you're looking to connect with other language enthusiasts through "Natura Lingua", we invite you to join our online group. In this community, you'll have the opportunity to ask questions, find learning partners, and share your progress.

- **Explore more with other Natura Lingua manuals:** If you like this method, note that there are other similar manuals for different languages. Discover our complete collection of manuals to enrich your linguistic learning experience in a natural and progressive way.

We are here to support you in learning the target language. For optimal results, we highly recommend downloading the audio and using the flashcards. These additional resources are designed to further facilitate your journey.

Happy learning!

GERMAN IN 100 DAYS

Check off a box below after completing each lesson.
This will aid you in monitoring your progress and
maintaining motivation throughout your learning
experience.

IMPORTANT NOTES :

1. **The Essentials: Vocabulary and Key Phrases:** In each Natura Lingua lesson, we carefully select the most useful words and expressions relevant to the theme studied. The goal is to familiarize you with the most frequently used constructions in the target language. Sometimes, the general meaning of the texts might seem surprising, but don't worry, it's an essential part of our method. It helps you focus on the practical aspects of the language, thereby accelerating your learning for better understanding and more effective communication.

2. **Translation: As Close to the Original as Possible:** We translate in a way that stays true to the source text, capturing how sentences are structured and ideas are conveyed in the target language. Our goal is not syntactic perfection in English, but rather to give you an authentic insight into the thought process and structure of the language you are learning. This method immerses you in the language, allowing you to gain a more natural and intuitive understanding. Our aim is to help you think and communicate fluently in the learned language, not just understand it. We want to prepare you to use the language practically and confidently in your daily life.

TAG NR. 1: BEGRÜSSUNGEN

1. Hallo!
2. Hi! Guten Morgen.
3. Guten Nachmittag.
4. Danke. Bis später.
5. Auf Wiedersehen. Gute Nacht.
6. Gern geschehen.

✤ In German, all nouns start with a capital letter, whether they are at the beginning of a sentence or not.

DAY 1: GREETINGS

1. Hello!
2. Hi! Good morning.
3. Good afternoon.
4. Thank you. See you later.
5. Goodbye. Good night.
6. You're welcome.

❖ In Germany, it's common to greet friends with a firm handshake, but cheek kissing is reserved for very close friends and family.

1. Guten Morgen! Ist das Ihr **kleiner** Hund?
2. **Ja**, das ist mein Hund. **Entschuldigung**, er ist sehr aktiv.
3. Kein Problem. Ist das ein **großes** Problem für Sie?
4. **Nein**, es ist **in Ordnung**. Er ist ein guter Hund.
5. **Ok**, das ist gut. **Bitte** passen Sie auf ihn auf.
6. **Ja**, natürlich. **Es tut mir leid** für die Unannehmlichkeiten.
7. Kein Problem. Auf Wiedersehen!
8. Auf Wiedersehen!

✤ In German, the verb always comes second in a statement but moves to the first position in a question.

1. Good morning! Is that your **little** dog?
2. **Yes,** that's my dog. **Sorry,** he's very active.
3. No problem. Is that a **big** problem for you?
4. **No,** it's **fine.** He's a good dog.
5. **Ok,** that's good. **Please** take care of him.
6. **Yes,** of course. **I'm sorry** for the inconvenience.
7. No problem. Goodbye!
8. Goodbye!

✤ In Germany, saying 'Ich drücke dir die Daumen' (I'm pressing my thumbs for you) means you're wishing someone good luck, originating from the medieval practice of pressing thumbs to ward off evil spirits.

1. Hallo, **wie heißt du?**
2. **Mein Name ist Anna. Und du?**
3. **Ich bin** Peter. **Wie geht es dir**, Anna?
4. **Mir geht's gut, danke! Wie alt bist du**, Peter?
5. **Ich bin 30 Jahre alt. Und du**, Anna?
6. **Ich bin 28 Jahre alt.**

❖ In German, adjectives change form to match the gender, case, and number of the noun they describe.

1. Hello, **what's your name?**
2. **My name is Anna. And you?**
3. **I'm** Peter. **How are you,** Anna?
4. **I'm good, thank you! How old are you,** Peter?
5. **I am 30 years old. And you,** Anna?
6. **I am 28 years old.**

❖ In Germany, it's customary to bring a small gift or a bottle of wine when invited to someone's home for the first time.

1. Hallo! Woher kommst du?
2. Hi! Ich komme aus Berlin. Und du?
3. Ich komme aus München. Wo wohnst du?
4. Ich wohne in Berlin. Was machst du beruflich?
5. Ich bin Arzt. Und du?
6. Ich bin Lehrerin. Was magst du?
7. Ich mag Musik und Sport. Und du?
8. Mir geht's gut, danke! Ich mag auch Musik. Freut mich, dich kennenzulernen!
9. Freut mich auch. Schönen Tag noch!

❖ In German, the definite article changes based on the gender and case of the noun, for example, "der" for masculine, "die" for feminine, "das" for neutral, and "die" for plural.

1. **Hello! Where are you from?**
2. **Hi! I'm from Berlin. And you?**
3. **I'm from Munich. Where do you live?**
4. **I live in Berlin. What do you do for a living?**
5. **I'm a doctor. And you?**
6. **I'm a teacher. What do you like?**
7. **I like music and sports. And you?**
8. **I'm good, thanks! I like music too. Nice to meet you!**
9. **Nice to meet you too. Have a nice day!**

❖ In Germany, it's common to exchange business cards at the beginning of a meeting as a formal gesture of sharing personal information.

1. **Hallo,** ich verstehe **nicht, wo die Bibliothek ist.** Ich gehe gerade zur Universität.
2. Ich weiß, **wo die Bibliothek ist.** Ich kann dir helfen.
3. **Danke, das ist sehr nett.** Ich brauche auch ein Buch für meine Klasse.
4. **Kein Problem.** Ich gebe dir mein altes Buch.
5. **Wirklich? Das ist toll!** Ich kaufe dir einen Kaffee als Dankeschön.
6. **Das ist nicht nötig, aber** ich möchte einen Kaffee. Danke!
7. **Ok, lass uns gehen.** Ich schaue nach dem Buch, wenn wir zurückkommen.
8. In Ordnung, lass uns gehen.

✤ In German, use "ein" for masculine and neuter nouns and "eine" for feminine nouns before a common verb to mean "a" or "an."

1. **Hello,** I don't understand **where the library is.** I'm going to the university right now.
2. I know **where the library is.** I can help you.
3. **Thank you, that's very kind.** I also need a book for my class.
4. **No problem.** I'll give you my old book.
5. **Really? That's great!** I'll buy you a coffee as a thank you.
6. **That's not necessary, but** I would like a coffee. Thank you!
7. **Ok, let's go.** I'll look for the book when we get back.
8. Alright, let's go.

✤ In German, the verb "verschlimmbessern" directly translates to "to make something worse in an attempt to improve it," humorously capturing the cultural acknowledgment of good intentions gone awry.

1. Guten Tag! Was für ein **Getränk** möchten Sie?
2. Ich **verstehe** nicht. Was haben Sie?
3. Wir haben **Tee, Kaffee, Bier, Wasser, Limonade, Saft, Wein und Milch**.
4. Ich **brauche** einen **Kaffee**, bitte.
5. Sehr gut. Ich **gehe** und mache Ihren **Kaffee**.
6. **Danke**!

♣ In German, the pronoun for "the beverage" changes based on its gender: "der" for masculine, "die" for feminine, and "das" for neutral.

DAY 6: BEVERAGES 🌱

1. Good day! What kind of **drink** would you like?
2. I **don't understand**. What do you have?
3. We have **tea, coffee, beer, water, lemonade, juice, wine**, and **milk**.
4. I **need** a **coffee**, please.
5. Very well. I'll go and make your **coffee**.
6. **Thank you**!

✣ In Germany, toasting with water is considered bad luck, as it's believed to wish death upon those you're drinking with.

Important Reminder Before Starting Lesson 7

* * *

Congratulations on your progress so far! You are about to embark on a crucial stage of your learning: Phase No. 2.

Please follow these instructions starting from lesson 7:

- For each lesson from No. 7 onward, first translate the text of that lesson (No. 7, No. 8, etc.) from the target language into English.
- Then, go back 6 lessons and translate the English version of that lesson's text from English back into the target language, without referring to the original text.
- Compare your translation with the original text of that lesson and adjust if necessary.
- Read the original text of that lesson out loud, while listening to the audio.

This new phase is designed to activate the vocabulary you have already assimilated. Keep up the momentum and enjoy this enriching new phase of your learning!

1. Woher kommst du?
2. Ich komme aus Berlin.
3. Wo wohnst du?
4. **Ich wohne in Hamburg. Es ist** kalt dort.
5. Was machst du beruflich?
6. **Ich bin Kellner. Ich serviere** heißen **Kaffee und** kaltes Bier.
7. **Ist das** gut oder **schlecht**?
8. Es ist **gut**. Ich mag meinen Job.

✤ In German, adjectives used as adverbs to describe how something is done do not change form, regardless of the gender or number of the noun they refer to.

DAY 7: DESCRIPTIVE ADJECTIVES I 🌱

1. Where are you from?
2. I'm from Berlin.
3. Where do you live?
4. **I live in Hamburg. It's** cold there.
5. What do you do for a living?
6. **I'm a waiter. I serve** hot coffee and **cold** beer.
7. **Is that** good **or** bad?
8. **It's** good. I like my job.

✤ In German literature, characters are often described as "wanderlustig," reflecting the cultural value placed on exploration and adventure.

1. Entschuldigung, wo ist die Bank?
2. **Die Bank ist** dort drüben. **Sie müssen** geradeaus gehen.
3. **Ist es** weit **von** hier?
4. **Nein, es ist nicht** weit. **Es ist ziemlich** nah.
5. Und wo ist das Café?
6. **Das Café ist** hier drüben. **Sie müssen nach** links gehen.
7. Und die Apotheke?
8. **Die Apotheke ist** dort. **Sie müssen nach** rechts gehen.
9. **Danke, ich** verstehe jetzt.
10. Gern geschehen!

❖ In German, to indicate a location, use "in" for enclosed spaces (like "in der Schule" for "in the school") and "auf" for open spaces (like "auf dem Platz" for "on the square").

1. Excuse me, where is the bank?
2. **The bank is** over there. **You need to go** straight ahead.
3. **Is it** far from **here**?
4. No, it's not **far**. It's quite **close**.
5. And where is the café?
6. **The café is** right here. **You need to go** left.
7. And the pharmacy?
8. **The pharmacy is** there. **You need to go** right.
9. **Thank you, I** understand now.
10. You're welcome!

❖ Neuschwanstein Castle, the inspiration for Disney's Sleeping Beauty Castle, was never fully completed.

1. Entschuldigung, wo ist das Café?
2. Gehen Sie **geradeaus** und dann **rechts abbiegen**. Es ist **auf der rechten Seite**.
3. Und wo ist die Toilette?
4. Die Toilette ist **hinter** dem Café.
5. Und wo kann ich mein Auto parken?
6. Sie können **hier parken**. Der Parkplatz ist **neben** dem Café.
7. Vielen Dank!
8. Gern geschehen!

❖ In German, when giving directions, we often use the conjunction "und" (and) to connect two instructions, like "Gehen Sie geradeaus und dann rechts." (Go straight and then right.)

1. Excuse me, where is the café?
2. Go **straight ahead** and then **turn right**. It is **on the right side**.
3. And where is the restroom?
4. The restroom is **behind** the café.
5. And where can I park my car?
6. You can **park here**. The parking lot is **next to** the café.
7. Thank you!
8. You're welcome!

✤ The Brandenburg Gate in Berlin was once part of a wall dividing the city and is now a symbol of unity and peace.

1. **Wo** ist das Museum?
2. Es ist **neben** dem Park.
3. **Wann** öffnet es?
4. Es öffnet um 10 Uhr. **Wie spät ist es** jetzt?
5. Es ist 9 Uhr. **Wie viel kostet das** Eintrittsticket?
6. Es kostet 15 Euro.
7. **Warum** ist es so **teuer**?
8. Weil es sehr **beliebt** ist.

✤ In German, to form a question, you often just need to move the verb to the beginning of the sentence.

1. **Where** is the museum?
2. It's **next to** the park.
3. **When** does it open?
4. It opens at 10 o'clock. **What time is it** now?
5. It's 9 o'clock. **How much does the** entrance ticket **cost**?
6. It costs 15 Euros.
7. **Why** is it so **expensive**?
8. Because it's very **popular**.

✤ In Germany, directness in asking questions is valued over beating around the bush, reflecting their appreciation for clarity and efficiency.

CHALLENGE NO. 1

CHOOSE A THEME AND CREATE A COLLAGE
OF PHOTOS OR IMAGES, NOTING THE
CORRESPONDING WORD IN GERMAN.

"Durchhalten ist der erste Schritt zum Erfolg."

"Perseverance is the first step to success."

1. Hallo! Wie geht es dir **heute**?
2. Hi! Mir geht es gut, danke. Und dir?
3. Mir geht es auch gut. Was machst du **jetzt**?
4. Ich schaue auf die **Uhr**. Es ist fast **Zeit** für meine **Stunde** Deutschunterricht.
5. Ah, interessant! Und was hast du **gestern** gemacht?
6. **Gestern** habe ich einen Film gesehen. Und **morgen** gehe ich einkaufen.
7. Und was ist mit **übermorgen**?
8. **Übermorgen** habe ich frei. Ich werde mich entspannen.
9. Das klingt gut. Auf Wiedersehen!
10. Auf Wiedersehen!

✤ In German, days of the week are capitalized and time expressions use 24-hour format.

1. Hello! How are you **today**?
2. Hi! I'm good, thanks. And you?
3. I'm also good. What are you doing **now**?
4. I'm looking at the **clock**. It's almost **time** for my German lesson **hour**.
5. Ah, interesting! And what did you do **yesterday**?
6. **Yesterday, I watched a movie. And tomorrow** I'm going shopping.
7. And what about **the day after tomorrow**?
8. **The day after tomorrow** I have off. I will relax.
9. That sounds good. Goodbye!
10. Goodbye!

✤ In Germany, being punctual is so valued that being even a few minutes late can be seen as disrespectful.

TAG NR. 12: WOCHENTAGE

1. **Guten Tag!** Welcher Tag ist heute?
2. **Heute ist** Montag.
3. Und morgen?
4. **Morgen ist** Dienstag.
5. **Und** übermorgen?
6. **Übermorgen ist** Mittwoch.
7. **Ok, danke. Und wann ist das** Wochenende?
8. **Das Wochenende ist am** Samstag **und** Sonntag.
9. Vielen Dank!

✤ In German, days of the week are always capitalized and they act as the subject in sentences like "Montag ist kalt." (Monday is cold).

DAY 12: DAYS OF THE WEEK 🌱

1. **Good day!** What day is it today?
2. **Today is** Monday.
3. And tomorrow?
4. **Tomorrow is** Tuesday.
5. **And** the day after tomorrow?
6. **The day after tomorrow is** Wednesday.
7. **Ok, thanks. And when is the** weekend?
8. **The weekend is on** Saturday **and** Sunday.
9. Thank you very much!

❖ In Germany, Wednesday is called "Mittwoch," meaning mid-week, directly reflecting its position as the middle of the workweek.

1. Hallo, **Mann**! Wie geht es deiner **Familie**?
2. Hallo, **Frau**! Meinen **Eltern** geht es gut, danke! Und deiner **Familie**?
3. Meine **Mutter** und mein **Vater** sind bei meinen **Großeltern**. Mein **Bruder** und meine **Schwester** sind zu Hause.
4. Und dein **Ehemann**?
5. Mein **Ehemann** ist bei den **Kindern**.

❖ In German, the direct object of a sentence, often a family member in this context, takes the accusative case.

1. Hello, **Man**! How is your **family**?
2. Hello, **Woman**! My **parents** are doing well, thank you! And your **family**?
3. My **mother** and my **father** are at my **grandparents'**. My **brother** and my **sister** are at home.
4. And your **husband**?
5. My **husband** is with the **children**.

❖ In Germany, it was once common for multiple generations to live under one roof, fostering a strong sense of community and family support.

1. Hallo **Cousin**! Wie geht es deiner **Tante** und deinem **Onkel**?
2. Hallo Anna! Sie geht es gut. Und wie geht es deinem **Neffen** und deiner **Nichte**?
3. Ihnen geht es auch gut. Sie spielen jetzt mit meinem **Enkel** und meiner **Enkelin**.
4. Das ist schön. Sind deine **Freunde** auch da?
5. Ja, und mein **Kollege** und mein **Partner** sind auch hier.
6. Das klingt nach einer großen Familie!
7. Ja, das ist es. Familie ist sehr wichtig für mich.

✤ In German, to show someone is receiving something or benefiting from an action, we often use the dative case for the indirect object, like in "Ich gebe meinem Bruder ein Geschenk" (I give my brother a present).

1. Hello **Cousin**! How are your **aunt** and **uncle** doing?
2. Hello Anna! They are doing well. And how is your **nephew** and **niece**?
3. They are also doing well. They are playing with my **grandson** and my **granddaughter** right now.
4. That's nice. Are your **friends** there too?
5. Yes, and my **colleague** and my **partner** are here as well.
6. That sounds like a big family!
7. Yes, it is. Family is very important to me.

❖ In Germany, a child's first day of school is celebrated with a "Schultüte," a large cone filled with sweets and gifts to make the start of their education journey a memorable one.

1. Hallo Peter, wie viele **Cousins** hast du?
2. Ich habe **zwei** Cousins.
3. Und wie viele **Tanten** und **Onkel** hast du?
4. Ich habe **drei** Tanten und **vier** Onkel.
5. Wow, das ist eine große Familie! Hast du auch **Neffen** oder **Nichten**?
6. Ja, ich habe **fünf** Neffen und **sechs** Nichten.
7. Das ist unglaublich! Und wann siehst du sie normalerweise?
8. Ich sehe sie normalerweise am **Samstag** und **Sonntag**.
9. Ich **verstehe**, danke für die Information, Peter!

❖ In German, when talking about the number of items in the present tense, the verb agrees with the subject in number and person, like "Ich habe zwei Bücher" (I have two books).

DAY 15: NUMBERS FROM 1 TO 10 🌱

1. Hello Peter, how many **cousins** do you have?
2. I have **two** cousins.
3. And how many **aunts** and **uncles** do you have?
4. I have **three** aunts and **four** uncles.
5. Wow, that's a big family! Do you also have **nephews** or **nieces**?
6. Yes, I have **five** nephews and **six** nieces.
7. That's incredible! And when do you usually see them?
8. I usually see them on **Saturday** and **Sunday**.
9. I **understand**, thanks for the information, Peter!

✤ In Germany, the number 13 is often considered lucky, contrary to many other cultures where it's seen as unlucky.

1. Hallo, **Mutter**. Wie viele **Brüder** habe ich?
2. Du hast einen **Bruder**, Anna.
3. Und wie viele **Schwestern** habe ich?
4. Du hast **zwölf** Schwestern, Anna.
5. Wow, das sind **dreizehn** Kinder insgesamt!
6. Ja, das ist richtig. Möchtest du etwas trinken? Tee, Kaffee, Bier, Wasser oder Limonade?
7. Ich nehme ein Glas **Wasser**, bitte.

✤ In German, numbers from 11 to 20 are used in the affirmative form by placing them directly before the noun they are quantifying, without changing their form.

1. Hello, **Mother**. How many **brothers** do I have?
2. You have one **brother**, Anna.
3. And how many **sisters** do I have?
4. You have **twelve** sisters, Anna.
5. Wow, that's **thirteen** children in total!
6. Yes, that's correct. Would you like something to drink? Tea, coffee, beer, water, or lemonade?
7. I'll have a glass of **water**, please.

❖ In Germany, the counting rhyme "Ene mene miste" is a popular way to decide who's "it" in games, tracing back to ancient counting methods.

1. Hallo Peter, willst du mit mir zum **Markt** gehen?
2. Ja, ich muss etwas im **Geschäft kaufen**.
3. Was willst du kaufen?
4. Ich **suche** nach einem neuen Hemd. Aber ich hoffe, es ist nicht zu **teuer**.
5. Vielleicht gibt es einen **Verkauf** oder einen **Rabatt**.
6. Das wäre toll. Soll ich mit **Bargeld** oder **Kreditkarte** bezahlen?
7. Das hängt vom Geschäft ab. Manche akzeptieren nur Bargeld.
8. Okay, danke für die Information.

✤ In German, to make sentences negative, add "nicht" or "kein" before the noun or verb you want to negate.

DAY 17: SHOPPING I

1. Hello Peter, do you want to go to the **market** with me?
2. Yes, I need to **buy** something at the **store**.
3. What do you want to buy?
4. I'm **looking** for a new shirt. But I hope it's not too **expensive**.
5. Maybe there's a **sale** or a **discount**.
6. That would be great. Should I pay with **cash** or **credit card**?
7. It depends on the store. Some only accept cash.
8. Okay, thanks for the information.

✤ In traditional German Christmas markets, haggling is often frowned upon, emphasizing fixed prices for a harmonious festive spirit.

1. Hallo, ich möchte diese **Jacke** und diese **Sonnenbrille kaufen. Wo ist die Kasse?**

2. Die **Kasse** ist **dort**. Brauchen Sie einen **Wagen** oder einen **Korb?**

3. Nein, danke. Das ist nicht nötig. Wie viel ist der **Preis?**

4. Die **Jacke** kostet fünfzig Euro und die **Sonnenbrille** zwanzig Euro.

5. Das ist nicht **teuer**. Ich nehme beides. Bitte geben Sie mir die **Quittung.**

6. Natürlich, hier ist Ihre **Quittung**. Vielen Dank für Ihren Einkauf!

❖ To ask how much something costs in German, you start with "Wie viel kostet" followed by the item.

1. Hello, I would like to **buy** this **jacket** and these **sunglasses**. Where is the **cash register**?
2. The **cash register** is **over there**. Do you need a **cart** or a **basket**?
3. No, thank you. That's not necessary. How much is the **price**?
4. The **jacket** costs fifty euros and the **sunglasses** twenty euros.
5. That's not **expensive**. I'll take both. Please give me the **receipt**.
6. Of course, here is your **receipt**. Thank you for your purchase!

✤ Germany is home to the world's oldest shopping mall, the "Alte Leipziger Messe," which dates back to the 16th century.

1. **Guten Morgen! Ich brauche ein** Taxi **zum** Flughafen.
2. Kein Problem. Wo sind Sie jetzt?
3. **Ich bin am** Bahnhof.
4. **Gut. Ein** Taxi kommt in fünfzehn Minuten.
5. **Danke. Ich fahre normalerweise mit dem** Bus oder **Auto**, aber heute ist mein **Auto** kaputt.
6. **Das ist schade. Haben Sie schon einmal mit dem** Fahrrad **oder** Zug gefahren?
7. Nein, das habe ich noch nicht. Vielleicht nächstes Mal.

✤ In German, to form a simple declarative sentence about transport, place the subject first, followed by the verb, and then the means of transport, for example, "Ich fahre mit dem Zug."

1. **Good morning! I need a** Taxi **to the** Airport.
2. No problem. Where are you now?
3. **I'm at the** Train Station.
4. **Good. A** Taxi will arrive in fifteen minutes.
5. **Thank you. I usually take the** Bus or **Car,** but today my **Car** is broken.
6. **That's unfortunate. Have you ever traveled by** Bicycle **or** Train?
7. No, I haven't. Maybe next time.

✤ In Germany, there's a suspended monorail system called the Wuppertal Schwebebahn, which has been in operation since 1901.

1. **Entschuldigung, wo ist das** Terminal **für die** Abfahrt?
2. **Welchen** Flugsteig suchen Sie?
3. **Ich habe meine** Boardingkarte verloren, aber ich weiß, dass mein Flug nach Berlin geht.
4. **Oh, das ist schlecht. Haben Sie Ihr** Gepäck schon eingecheckt?
5. **Ja, ich habe nur meinen** Rucksack **und meinen** Koffer dabei.
6. **Ihr Flug ist leider** verspätet. **Sie können eine neue** Boardingkarte am Schalter kaufen.
7. Vielen Dank für Ihre Hilfe.

✤ To ask about transportation in German, start your question with "Wie" for "How" or "Wo" for "Where", followed by the verb and subject.

1. **Excuse me, where is the** departure terminal?
2. **Which** gate are you looking for?
3. **I've lost my** boarding pass, but I know my flight is going to Berlin.
4. **Oh, that's bad. Have you already checked in your** luggage?
5. **Yes, I only have my** backpack **and my** suitcase with me.
6. **Unfortunately, your flight is** delayed. **You can buy a new** boarding pass at the counter.
7. Thank you for your help.

✤ In 1881, the world's first electric tram went into operation in Berlin, Germany, marking a significant milestone in the history of public transport.

CHALLENGE NO. 2

WRITE A SHORT TEXT IN GERMAN
INTRODUCING YOURSELF AND
EXPLAINING WHY YOU ARE LEARNING
THIS LANGUAGE.

"Lernen ist wie Rudern gegen den Strom. Sobald man
aufhört, treibt man zurück."
"Learning is like rowing against the current. As soon as
you stop, you drift back."

1. Hallo Peter, wo warst du **gestern**?
2. Ich war im **Büro** und dann in der **Schule**. Und du?
3. Ich war im **Krankenhaus** und dann in der **Apotheke**.
4. Und wo gehst du **heute** hin?
5. Ich gehe zur **Bank** und dann ins **Restaurant**.
6. Und **morgen**?
7. **Morgen gehe ich ins Hotel und dann in die Bar**.
8. Und übermorgen?
9. **Übermorgen** gehe ich in den **Park**.

✤ To give directions in German using the imperative, simply use the verb at the beginning of the sentence, like "Gehen Sie geradeaus!" (Go straight ahead!).

1. Hello Peter, where were you **yesterday**?
2. I was at the **office** and then at **school**. And you?
3. I was at the **hospital** and then at the **pharmacy**.
4. And where are you going **today**?
5. I'm going to the **bank** and then to the **restaurant**.
6. And **tomorrow**?
7. **Tomorrow I'm going to the hotel and then to the bar**.
8. And the day after tomorrow?
9. **The day after tomorrow I'm going to the park**.

✤ Germany's Neuschwanstein Castle, a World Heritage Site, inspired Disney's Sleeping Beauty Castle.

1. Guten Morgen, Peter. Wie war dein **Montag**?
2. Es war **lang** und **laut** im **Büro**. Und dein Tag?
3. Mein Tag war **kurz** aber **schnell**. Ich war im **Krankenhaus** und in der **Apotheke**.
4. Das klingt **sehr** anstrengend. Wie bist du dorthin gekommen?
5. Ich habe ein **Taxi** genommen. Es war **wenig** Verkehr heute.
6. Das ist gut. Ich hoffe, dein **Dienstag** ist **besser** und **ruhig**.

✤ In exclamatory sentences using adjectives in German, place the adjective before the noun and add "wie" or "so" before the adjective to express strong feelings, like "Wie schön der Tag ist!"

1. Good morning, Peter. How was your **Monday**?
2. It was **long** and **loud** in the **office**. And your day?
3. My day was **short** but **fast**. I was at the **hospital** and the **pharmacy**.
4. That sounds **very** exhausting. How did you get there?
5. I took a **taxi**. There was **little** traffic today.
6. That's good. I hope your **Tuesday** is **better** and **quiet**.

❖ Germany's Black Forest inspired the fairy tales of the Brothers Grimm.

1. Ist das Wasser **warm** oder **kalt**?
2. Es ist **kalt**, aber nicht **nass**.
3. Ist dein Brötchen **hart** oder **weich**?
4. Es ist **hart**. Und der Kuchen ist **leicht** und **trocken**.
5. Ist dein Zimmer **voll** oder leer?
6. Es ist **voll**. Es ist **schwer**, alles zu organisieren.
7. Ist es **still** in deinem Zimmer?
8. Ja, es ist sehr **still**.

✤ In negative sentences, adjectives do not change form.

1. Is the water **warm** or **cold**?
2. It's **cold**, but not **wet**.
3. Is your roll **hard** or **soft**?
4. It's **hard**. And the cake is **light** and **dry**.
5. Is your room **full** or empty?
6. It's **full**. It's **hard** to organize everything.
7. Is it **quiet** in your room?
8. Yes, it's very **quiet**.

✤ German poets often use compound adjectives, creating vivid and unique imagery in just a few words.

TAG NR. 24: FARBEN 🌱

1. Hallo **Onkel** Peter, wie geht es dir?
2. Hallo **Anna**, mir geht es gut. Ich bin gerade im **Büro**. Und dir?
3. Mir geht es auch gut. Ich bin in der **Schule**. Wir lernen heute die **Farben**.
4. Das ist interessant. Welche **Farben** lernst du?
5. Wir lernen **Rot, Blau, Grün, Gelb, Schwarz, Weiß, Braun, Rosa, Grau und Orange**.
6. Das sind viele **Farben**. Viel Spaß beim Lernen, **Anna**!
7. Danke, **Onkel** Peter!

✤ In German, the names of colors are not capitalized unless they are at the beginning of a sentence.

1. Hello **Uncle** Peter, how are you?
2. Hello **Anna**, I'm doing well. I'm currently at the **office**. And you?
3. I'm also doing well. I'm at **school**. Today, we're learning about **colors**.
4. That's interesting. Which **colors** are you learning?
5. We're learning **Red, Blue, Green, Yellow, Black, White, Brown, Pink, Gray**, and **Orange**.
6. That's a lot of **colors**. Have fun learning, **Anna**!
7. Thank you, **Uncle** Peter!

✤ In Germany, a white sausage must never be eaten after noon, symbolizing its freshness and tradition.

1. **Hallo, kannst du mir helfen? Mein** Computer funktioniert nicht.
2. Natürlich, was ist das Problem?
3. **Ich kann keine** E-Mails **senden und das** Internet ist sehr langsam.
4. **Hast du schon versucht, das** WLAN neu zu starten?
5. **Ja, aber es hat nicht geholfen. Auch mein** Smartphone **kann keine** Apps herunterladen.
6. **Vielleicht solltest du einen anderen** Browser **versuchen. Oder dein** Laptop könnte ein Update benötigen.
7. Das ist eine gute Idee. Danke für deine Hilfe.
8. Kein Problem, auf Wiedersehen!

✤ In German, always use a comma before a subordinate clause, which often starts with words like "dass" (that) or "weil" (because), even when talking about electronics and technology.

1. **Hello, can you help me? My** Computer is not working.
2. Of course, what's the problem?
3. **I can't send** E-Mails **and the** Internet is very slow.
4. **Have you tried restarting the** WLAN?
5. **Yes, but it didn't help. Also, my** Smartphone **can't** download **any** Apps.
6. **Maybe you should try a different** Browser. **Or your** Laptop might need an update.
7. That's a good idea. Thanks for your help.
8. No problem, goodbye!

♣ The MP3 format, revolutionizing digital music, was invented by German engineer Karl-heinz Brandenburg.

1. Hallo Peter, wann hast du Geburtstag?
2. Ich habe im **Juli** Geburtstag. Und du?
3. Mein Geburtstag ist im **Oktober**. Welcher Monat ist dein Lieblingsmonat?
4. Mein Lieblingsmonat ist der **Mai**. Es ist warm, aber nicht zu heiß. Und deiner?
5. Ich mag den **April**. Es ist nicht zu kalt und nicht zu warm.

✤ In German, to talk about past events in months or seasons, use the simple past tense for regular verbs by adding "-te" to the stem for most verbs, like "Ich reiste im Sommer" (I traveled in the summer).

1. Hello Peter, when is your birthday?
2. My birthday is in **July**. And yours?
3. My birthday is in **October**. Which month is your favorite?
4. My favorite month is **May**. It's warm, but not too hot. And yours?
5. I like **April**. It's not too cold and not too warm.

✤ In Germany, the Oktoberfest originally started as a royal wedding celebration in 1810 and has since evolved into the world's largest beer festival.

1. Guten Tag! Wie ist die **Vorhersage** für **November** und **Dezember**?
2. Es wird viel **Regen** im **November** geben und der **Dezember** wird wie der **Winter** sein.
3. Und wie wird das **Klima** im **Frühling** und **Sommer**?
4. Der **Frühling** wird voller **Sonnenschein** sein und der **Sommer** wird wie der **Herbst** sein.
5. Danke für die Informationen!

✤ To talk about future events in German, you can use "werden" plus the infinitive of the verb, as in "Im Sommer werden wir schwimmen gehen" (In the summer, we will go swimming).

1. Good day! What is the **forecast** for **November** and **December**?
2. There will be a lot of **rain** in **November** and **December** will be like **winter**.
3. And what will the **climate** be like in **spring** and **summer**?
4. **Spring will be full of sunshine and summer will be like autumn**.
5. Thank you for the information!

❖ In Germany, people hide pickles in their Christmas trees, and the first child to find it gets a special gift.

1. Hallo, wie geht es dir heute?
2. **Ich bin** glücklich **und** fröhlich. Und du?
3. **Ich bin ein bisschen** nervös **und** aufgeregt. Ich habe morgen einen großen Test.
4. Oh, das verstehe ich. Bist du gut vorbereitet?
5. **Ja, ich denke schon. Aber ich bin immer noch** besorgt.
6. **Mach dir keine Sorgen. Du wirst großartig sein. Ich bin** stolz auf dich.
7. Danke, das bedeutet mir viel.

✤ In German, the indicative mood is used to express facts and real situations, like "Ich bin glücklich" (I am happy).

1. Hello, how are you today?
2. **I am** happy **and** cheerful. And you?
3. **I'm a bit** nervous **and** excited. I have a big test tomorrow.
4. Oh, I understand that. Are you well prepared?
5. **Yes, I think so. But I'm still** worried.
6. **Don't worry. You'll be great. I'm** proud of you.
7. Thank you, that means a lot to me.

✤ In Germany, it's common to knock on the table instead of clapping to show appreciation in academic settings, expressing respect and emotion uniquely.

1. Hallo, **Mai**. Wie geht es dir heute? Bist du **gestresst**?

2. Hallo, **Jan**. Ja, ich bin ein bisschen **verwirrt** und **ängstlich**. Ich **vermisse dich**.

3. Oh, das tut mir leid zu hören. Warum bist du **verärgert**?

4. Ich **habe** ein **Taxi** zum **Flughafen** gebraucht, aber ich **verstehe** die Wegbeschreibung nicht.

5. Keine Sorge, **Mai**. Ich **gehe** mit dir zum **Flughafen**.

6. Wirklich? Oh, das macht mich **erfreut** und **zufrieden. Ich liebe dich, Jan**.

7. Ich auch, **Mai. Ich mache nur Spaß**.

✤ In German, to give commands or instructions, we use the imperative mood by taking the verb's stem for "du" (drop the "st" and add "e" if it ends in "d" or "t"), use the verb as is for "ihr", and add "en" or "n" to the infinitive for "Sie" and "wir".

1. Hello, **Mai**. How are you today? Are you **stressed**?
2. Hello, **Jan**. Yes, I'm a bit **confused** and **anxious**. I **miss you**.
3. Oh, I'm sorry to hear that. Why are you **upset**?
4. I **needed** a **taxi to the airport, but I don't understand** the directions.
5. Don't worry, **Mai**. I'll **go** with you to the **airport**.
6. Really? Oh, that makes me **happy** and **satisfied**. I **love you**, Jan.
7. I love you too, **Mai**. **I'm just kidding**.

✤ Rainer Maria Rilke, a renowned German poet, penned the timeless "Letters to a Young Poet," offering profound insights on love and creativity.

1. Hallo, wie geht es dir?
2. **Mein** Kopf **tut weh und meine** Nase ist verstopft.
3. Oh nein, das klingt nicht gut. Hast du Fieber?
4. **Nein, aber mein** Mund **ist trocken. Kannst du mir bitte ein Glas** Wasser bringen?
5. Natürlich, ich bringe es sofort.

✤ To express a wish or hypothetical situation about body parts, use the subjunctive mood by adding "wäre" (were) or "hätte" (had), as in "Ich wünschte, ich hätte größere Hände" (I wish I had bigger hands).

1. Hello, how are you?
2. **My** head **hurts and my** nose is stuffed up.
3. Oh no, that doesn't sound good. Do you have a fever?
4. **No, but my** mouth **is dry. Can you please bring me a glass of** water?
5. Of course, I'll bring it right away.

✤ In Germany, the traditional Bavarian dress, Dirndl, is designed to flatter and accentuate the female figure, showcasing the importance of beauty and body image in cultural attire.

CHALLENGE NO. 3

CHOOSE A SHORT ARTICLE IN A GERMAN NEWSPAPER AND TRANSLATE IT INTO ENGLISH.

"Reden ist Silber, Schweigen ist Gold."

"Talking is silver, silence is golden."

1. Hallo, wie geht es dir?
2. **Mir geht es** gut, danke. Aber mein **Fuß** tut weh.
3. Oh nein, was ist passiert?
4. **Ich bin schnell gelaufen und habe mein** Knie gestoßen.
5. **Das klingt** schlecht. **Vielleicht solltest du ins** Krankenhaus gehen.
6. Ja, das ist eine gute Idee. Ich hoffe, es ist nichts Ernstes.
7. Ich hoffe auch. Pass auf dich auf!

❖ If you were a doctor, you would need to know all the body parts in German to explain conditions to patients.

1. Hello, how are you?
2. **I'm** good, **thank you. But my** foot hurts.
3. Oh no, what happened?
4. **I was running fast and I bumped my** knee.
5. **That sounds** bad. Maybe you should go to the **hospital**.
6. Yes, that's a good idea. I hope it's nothing serious.
7. I hope so too. Take care of yourself!

✤ In Germany, the Bavarian Schuhplattler dance involves performers slapping their shoes and knees to mimic the courtship display of the Auerhahn bird.

1. **Guten** Tag! Wie geht es deinem **Zeitplan** für die **Woche**?
2. Er ist sehr voll. Ich habe jeden **Tag** etwas zu tun.
3. **Und wie ist dein** Monat?
4. **Er ist auch sehr beschäftigt. Jede** Minute zählt.
5. **Und das** Jahr?
6. Es ist noch zu früh, um zu sagen. Aber ich hoffe, es wird gut.
7. **Ich hoffe es auch. Lass uns in der** Nacht sprechen.
8. Ja, das ist eine gute Idee. Bis später!

✤ In German, when talking about time and calendar in the active voice, the subject performs the action, like "Der Zug kommt um 10 Uhr an" (The train arrives at 10 o'clock).

DAY 32: TIME AND CALENDAR 🌱

1. **Good** day! How is your **schedule** for the **week**?
2. It's very full. I have something to do every **day**.
3. And how about your **month**?
4. It's also very busy. Every **minute** counts.
5. **And the** year?
6. It's too early to tell. But I hope it will be good.
7. **I hope so too. Let's talk in the** night.
8. Yes, that's a good idea. See you later!

♣ In Germany, the Advent calendar, a tradition since the 19th century, counts down the days to Christmas with little doors hiding sweets or gifts.

1. **Guten Morgen! Möchtest du** Tee oder **Kaffee** zum Frühstück?
2. **Ich nehme einen Kaffee, bitte. Und etwas** Brot.
3. **Möchtest du auch ein** Ei dazu?
4. **Ja, bitte. Und hast du auch** Obst?
5. Ja, wir haben Äpfel und Bananen.
6. **Perfekt! Ich liebe** Obst am Morgen.
7. **Und zum Mittagessen?** Fleisch, Gemüse, Reis **oder** Nudeln?
8. **Ich nehme** Gemüse **und** Reis, bitte.
9. **Sehr gut. Und zum Trinken? Wasser,** Tee **oder** Bier?
10. **Ein** Bier, bitte.

❖ In German, to form the passive voice for sentences about food, you often use "werden" plus the past participle of the verb, as in "Die Pizza wird gegessen" (The pizza is being eaten).

1. **Good morning! Would you like** tea or **coffee** for breakfast?
2. **I'll have a coffee, please. And some** bread.
3. **Would you like an** egg with that?
4. **Yes, please. And do you have any** fruit?
5. Yes, we have apples and bananas.
6. **Perfect! I love** fruit in the morning.
7. **And for lunch?** Meat, vegetables, rice, **or** pasta?
8. **I'll have** vegetables **and** rice, please.
9. **Very good. And to drink? Water,** tea, **or** beer?
10. A beer, please.

✤ In Germany, the Döner Kebab, originally from Turkey, has become so popular that it's considered by many as a national dish, rivaling even the traditional Bratwurst.

1. Guten Morgen, Peter. Was möchtest du zum Frühstück? Ein **Sandwich** mit **Butter** und **Käse**?
2. Nein, danke. Ich hätte lieber eine **Suppe** mit **Hähnchen** und **Gemüse**.
3. Ok, und zum Trinken? **Tee, Kaffee oder Bier**?
4. **Kaffee**, bitte. Und hast du auch einen **Kuchen**?
5. Ja, ich habe einen Apfelkuchen gemacht.

✤ In German, to talk about the circumstances of eating, like where or with whom, use prepositions like "mit" for with or "bei" for at, followed by the appropriate case.

1. Good morning, Peter. What would you like for breakfast? A **sandwich** with **butter** and **cheese**?
2. No, thank you. I would prefer a **soup** with **chicken** and **vegetables**.
3. Ok, and to drink? **Tea, coffee, or beer?**
4. **Coffee**, please. And do you have a **cake**?
5. Yes, I made an apple pie.

✤ In Germany, the pretzel has a religious origin, symbolizing arms crossed in prayer, and was given to children as a reward for learning prayers.

1. Guten Tag, was möchten Sie trinken? **Limonade, Wasser, Wein oder Saft?**
2. Ich hätte gerne eine **Limonade**, bitte.
3. Sehr gut. Und zum Dessert? **Schokolade, Eiscreme, Kuchen oder Gebäck?**
4. Ich nehme ein Stück **Kuchen** und eine Kugel **Eiscreme**.
5. Perfekt. Ihre Bestellung kommt gleich.

❖ In German, when talking about drinks and desserts, each independent clause can stand alone as a complete sentence, like "Ich trinke Kaffee, und sie isst Kuchen."

DAY 35: DRINKS AND DESSERTS 🌱

1. Good day, what would you like to drink?
   Lemonade, Water, Wine, or **Juice**?
2. I would like a **Lemonade**, please.
3. Very good. And for dessert? **Chocolate, Ice Cream, Cake**, or **Pastry**?
4. I'll have a slice of **Cake** and a scoop of **Ice Cream**.
5. Perfect. Your order will be right up.

❖ The Black Forest cake was named after the specialty liquor of the Black Forest region in Germany, not the forest itself.

TAG NR. 36: KOCHEN UND KÜCHE 🌱

1. Guten Morgen! Was gibt es zum Frühstück?
2. Ich habe Brot **gebacken** im **Ofen**. Es gibt auch Butter und Marmelade im **Kühlschrank**.
3. Super! Ich hole die **Teller, Gabeln, Löffel und Messer**.
4. Möchtest du Kaffee oder Tee?
5. Ich nehme einen Kaffee, bitte. Und du?
6. Ich trinke lieber Tee am Morgen.

✤ In sentences about cooking and the kitchen, use a subordinate clause to add information, like "Ich koche, weil ich hungrig bin" (I cook because I am hungry), where "weil ich hungrig bin" is the subordinate clause explaining why.

1. Good morning! What's for breakfast?
2. I **baked** some bread in the **oven**. There's also butter and jam in the **fridge**.
3. Great! I'll get the **plates, forks, spoons**, and **knives**.
4. Would you like coffee or tea?
5. I'll have a coffee, please. And you?
6. I prefer tea in the morning.

✤ German chef Alfons Schuhbeck spices up traditional Bavarian cuisine with exotic herbs and flavors, showcasing culinary innovation.

1. Wo möchtest du in den Sommerferien hinfahren?
2. **Ich möchte an den** Strand **gehen und das** Meer sehen.
3. **Warum nicht in die** Berge **oder in den** Wald?
4. **Ich mag auch den** Fluss **und die** Insel. **Aber ich mag keine** Wüste **oder den** Dschungel.
5. **Und das** Tal?
6. **Das** Tal ist auch schön. Aber der **Strand** ist mein Favorit.

✤ In German, to create a complex sentence about travel or places, you can connect two ideas using conjunctions like "weil" (because) or "obwohl" (although), placing the verb at the end of the subordinate clause.

1. Where would you like to go for the summer holidays?
2. **I want to go to the** beach **and see the** sea.
3. **Why not to the** mountains **or into the** forest?
4. **I also like the** river **and the** island. **But I don't like the** desert **or the** jungle.
5. **And the** valley?
6. **The** valley **is also beautiful. But the** beach is my favorite.

❖ Alexander von Humboldt's extensive travels and studies laid the foundation for the field of biogeography.

1. Hallo **Onkel** Peter, wie geht es dir?
2. Nicht so gut, Anna. Ich brauche **Hilfe**. Ich habe eine **Verletzung**.
3. Oh nein! Soll ich die **Polizei** oder das **Krankenhaus** anrufen?
4. Nein, es ist nicht so schlimm. Ich brauche nur etwas **Medizin**.
5. Okay, ich hole dir eine **Pille**. Du solltest auch zum **Arzt** gehen.
6. Ja, du hast recht. Ich werde morgen zum **Arzt** gehen.

✤ In German, the gender of nouns related to emergencies and health, like "der Arzt" (the doctor) for masculine and "die Krankheit" (the illness) for feminine, affects the articles and adjectives used with them.

1. Hello **Uncle** Peter, how are you?
2. Not so good, Anna. I need **help**. I have an **injury**.
3. Oh no! Should I call the **police** or the **hospital**?
4. No, it's not that bad. I just need some **medicine**.
5. Okay, I'll get you a **pill**. You should also see a **doctor**.
6. Yes, you're right. I will go to the **doctor** tomorrow.

♣ Germany introduced the world's first national health system in 1883.

1. Hallo Peter, wie alt bist du?
2. Ich bin **einundzwanzig** Jahre alt. Und du?
3. Ich bin **zweiundzwanzig**. Hast du Geschwister?
4. Ja, ich habe **drei** Geschwister.
5. Wow, das ist eine große Familie! Wie fühlst du dich dabei?
6. Manchmal bin ich **gestresst**, aber meistens bin ich **erfreut**.

❖ In German, when using numbers 21-30 in a sentence, make sure the noun they describe matches in number and case, like in "23 Hunde spielen im Park" (23 dogs are playing in the park).

1. Hello Peter, how old are you?
2. I am **twenty-one** years old. And you?
3. I am **twenty-two**. Do you have any siblings?
4. Yes, I have **three** siblings.
5. Wow, that's a big family! How do you feel about it?
6. Sometimes I'm **stressed**, but mostly I'm **delighted**.

❖ In Germany, the first recorded lottery to distribute prize money occurred in Hamburg in 1614.

1. **Guten Morgen! Was hast du** gestern gemacht?
2. **Ich war am** Strand. Und du?
3. **Ich war im** Wald. **Was machst du** heute?
4. **Ich gehe zum** Berg. Und morgen?
5. Morgen **gehe ich zum** Fluss. **Was ist mit dem** Montag?
6. **Am** Montag **gehe ich zum** Meer. **Und am** Dienstag?
7. **Am** Dienstag bleibe ich zu Hause.

✤ In German, when comparing days of the week, we use "als" for "than" to say one day is earlier or later than another, like "Montag ist früher als Mittwoch" (Monday is earlier than Wednesday).

1. **Good morning! What did you do** yesterday?
2. **I was at the** beach. And you?
3. **I was in the** forest. **What are you doing** today?
4. **I'm going to the** mountain. And tomorrow?
5. Tomorrow **I'm going to the** river. **What about** Monday?
6. **On** Monday **I'm going to the** sea. **And on** Tuesday?
7. **On** Tuesday I'm staying at home.

✤ In Germany, it's considered bad luck to celebrate birthdays before the actual date, stemming from old myths that it tempts fate.

CHALLENGE NO. 4

WRITE A LETTER OR EMAIL IN GERMAN TO A FICTIONAL OR REAL FRIEND.

"Der beste Zeitpunkt für Veränderung ist jetzt."

"The best time for change is now."

1. Guten Morgen, Peter. Wo ist das **Sofa**?
2. Das Sofa ist neben dem **Tisch** und dem **Stuhl**.
3. Und wo ist das **Bett**?
4. Das Bett ist im **Badezimmer**. Nein, das ist ein Witz! Das Bett ist im Schlafzimmer.
5. Und die **Küche**?
6. Die Küche ist neben dem **Badezimmer**. Dort sind auch die **Lampe**, die **Tür**, das **Fenster** und die **Wand**.

❖ In German, to form the superlative of most adjectives, add "-st" or "-est" to the end of the adjective and use "am" before it, like "am größten" for "the biggest."

1. Good morning, Peter. Where is the **sofa**?
2. The sofa is next to the **table** and the **chair**.
3. And where is the **bed**?
4. The bed is in the **bathroom**. No, that's a joke! The bed is in the bedroom.
5. And the **kitchen**?
6. The kitchen is next to the **bathroom**. There are also the **lamp**, the **door**, the **window**, and the **wall**.

✦ In Germany, there's a unique spring cleaning tradition called "Frühjahrsputz," where homes are thoroughly cleaned to welcome the new season.

1. Hallo Peter, wie ist dein neues **Haus**?

2. Hallo Anna, es ist großartig! Es hat vier **Zimmer**, einen **Garten** und eine **Garage**.

3. Das klingt toll! Hat es auch einen **Balkon**?

4. Ja, es hat einen **Balkon** und eine schöne **Treppe** zum **Dach**.

5. Und wie sieht der **Boden** im Wohnzimmer aus?

6. Der **Boden** ist aus Holz und die **Decke** ist sehr hoch. Es ist ein sehr gemütliches **Haus**.

✤ In German, to form the comparative, we often add "-er" to the adjective, and for the superlative, we use "am" before the adjective and add "-sten" at the end, or "-esten" if the adjective ends in "d", "t", "s", "ß", "z", "sch", "x", or "tz".

1. Hello Peter, how is your new **house**?
2. Hello Anna, it's great! It has four **rooms**, a **garden**, and a **garage**.
3. That sounds wonderful! Does it also have a **balcony**?
4. Yes, it has a **balcony** and a beautiful **staircase** to the **roof**.
5. And what does the **floor** in the living room look like?
6. The **floor** is made of wood and the **ceiling** is very high. It's a very cozy **house**.

✤ In Germany, the first electric refrigerator for home use was invented by Miele in 1927, revolutionizing food storage.

1. Hallo Peter, wo ist das **Taxi**?
2. Es ist **hier, neben dem Auto**.
3. Und wo ist der **Bahnhof**?
4. Der Bahnhof ist **dort, hinter dem großen Haus**.
5. Ist das **Restaurant links oder rechts**?
6. Es ist **rechts, zwischen dem Garten und dem Flughafen**.
7. Und wo ist unser **Zimmer**?
8. Unser Zimmer ist **oben, in der Wohnung**.

✤ In German, when describing direction towards a place, use "nach" for cities and countries, and "zu" for specific locations like buildings.

1. Hello Peter, where is the **taxi**?
2. It's **here, next to the car**.
3. And where is the **train station**?
4. The train station is **there, behind the big house**.
5. Is the **restaurant left or right**?
6. It's **right, between the garden and the airport**.
7. And where is our **room**?
8. Our room is **upstairs, in the apartment**.

✤ In the 19th century, German explorer Alexander von Humboldt's detailed mapping of South America laid the groundwork for modern geographical science.

1. Hallo Peter, wo gehst du hin?
2. Ich gehe zum **Einkaufszentrum**. Ich muss zum **Supermarkt** und zum **Lebensmittelgeschäft**.
3. Vergiss nicht, einen **Korb** zu nehmen.
4. Ja, und ich muss auch an der **Kasse** bezahlen.
5. Hast du eine **Rückerstattung** für etwas?
6. Nein, aber ich hoffe, einen guten **Preis** zu bekommen. Vielleicht gibt es einen **Rabatt** oder einen **Verkauf**.
7. Vergiss nicht, die **Quittung** zu nehmen.

✤ In German, when asking a question, the verb comes before the subject.

1. Hello Peter, where are you going?
2. I'm going to the **shopping center**. I need to go to the **supermarket** and the **grocery store**.
3. Don't forget to take a **basket**.
4. Yes, and I also need to pay at the **checkout**.
5. Do you have a **refund** for something?
6. No, but I hope to get a good **price**. Maybe there's a **discount** or a **sale**.
7. Don't forget to take the **receipt**.

✤ In Germany, it's considered bad luck to give knives as gifts, as it's believed to sever the friendship.

1. **Guten Tag, ich möchte diese** Münze **und** Bargeld **wechseln. Was ist der** Wechselkurs?
2. **Der Wechselkurs ist heute gut. Sie können es am** Geldautomaten wechseln.
3. **Danke. Kann ich hier auch mit** Debitkarte **oder** Kreditkarte bezahlen?
4. **Ja, Sie können mit beiden bezahlen. Hier ist Ihre** Rechnung.
5. **Ich möchte auch etwas** kaufen **und** verkaufen. Wo kann ich das machen?
6. **Sie können im** Einkaufszentrum **oder im** Supermarkt einkaufen und verkaufen.

✤ In German, the verb comes second in a main clause but moves to the end in a subordinate clause, especially important when talking about transactions or costs.

1. **Good day, I would like to exchange this** coin **and** cash. **What is the** exchange rate?
2. **The exchange rate is good today. You can exchange it at the** ATM.
3. **Thank you. Can I also pay here with a** debit card **or** credit card?
4. **Yes, you can pay with both. Here is your** bill.
5. **I would also like to** buy **and** sell something. Where can I do that?
6. **You can** shop **and sell at the** shopping mall **or** supermarket.

✤ In medieval Germany, people used beer as a form of currency to pay their debts.

1. Guten Morgen, Peter. Wie ist die **Wetter**vorhersage für heute?
2. Es wird **feucht**. Es gibt eine Chance auf **Donner** und **Blitze**.
3. Oh, kein **Sonnenschein**?
4. Nein, es wird eher **Nieselregen** geben. Aber vielleicht sehen wir eine **Wolke** und einen **Regenbogen**.
5. Und keine **Schneeflocken**?
6. Nein, es ist zu warm für Schnee.

✤ In German, adjectives describing weather and nature often change their endings based on the gender, case, and number of the nouns they describe.

1. Good morning, Peter. What's the **weather** forecast for today?
2. It's going to be **humid**. There's a chance of **thunder** and **lightning**.
3. Oh, no **sunshine**?
4. No, it's more likely to be **drizzling**. But maybe we'll see a **cloud** and a **rainbow**.
5. And no **snowflakes**?
6. No, it's too warm for snow.

✤ In Germany, it's said that the mythical Lorelei, a siren, sits atop a rock on the Rhine River, luring sailors to their doom with her enchanting song.

1. Guten Morgen, Peter. Hast du die **Vorhersage** für das **Wetter** gesehen?
2. Ja, es wird ein **Sturm** erwartet. Es könnte sogar ein **Tornado** oder **Hurrikan** sein.
3. Oh nein! Das klingt wie eine **Katastrophe**. Ich hoffe, es gibt kein **Erdbeben** oder einen ausbrechenden **Vulkan**.
4. Das hoffe ich auch. Ich gehe jetzt zum **Lebensmittelgeschäft**. Wir brauchen mehr Vorräte.
5. Gute Idee. Vergiss nicht, einen **Korb** zu nehmen und an der **Kasse** zu bezahlen.
6. Natürlich nicht, Anna. Bleib **ruhig** und sicher hier.

✤ In German, the pronunciation of "ch" changes based on geography: after "e" and "i" it sounds like a hiss, but after "a," "o," "u," and "au" it's more like a throaty growl.

DAY 47: DISASTERS AND GEOGRAPHY 🌱

1. Good morning, Peter. Have you seen the **forecast** for the **weather**?
2. Yes, a **storm** is expected. It could even be a **tornado** or **hurricane**.
3. Oh no! That sounds like a **disaster**. I hope there's no **earthquake** or an erupting **volcano**.
4. I hope so too. I'm going to the **grocery store** now. We need more supplies.
5. Good idea. Don't forget to take a **basket** and to pay at the **checkout**.
6. Of course not, Anna. Stay **calm** and safe here.

✤ In Germany, the legendary town of Vineta is said to have been swallowed by the sea as divine punishment for its people's hubris.

1. Hallo Peter, was ist deine Lieblingsfarbe?
2. Meine Lieblingsfarbe ist **Blau**. Und deine?
3. Ich mag **Rot** sehr. Aber ich mag auch **Grün** und **Gelb**.
4. Und welche Farben magst du nicht?
5. Ich mag **Schwarz** und **Weiß** nicht so sehr. Sie sind zu einfach.
6. Verstehe. Wie findest du **Rosa** und **Braun**?
7. **Rosa** ist schön, aber **Braun** ist nicht meine Farbe. Und **Grau**?
8. **Grau ist okay. Aber Gold** ist besser!

✤ In German, the pronunciation of color names can change slightly depending on the gender of the noun they describe.

1. Hello Peter, what's your favorite color?
2. My favorite color is **Blue**. And yours?
3. I really like **Red**. But I also like **Green** and **Yellow**.
4. And which colors do you not like?
5. I don't like **Black** and **White** that much. They're too simple.
6. I see. What do you think about **Pink** and **Brown**?
7. **Pink** is nice, but **Brown** is not my color. And **Gray**?
8. **Gray is okay. But Gold** is better!

✤ In Germany, the Holi Festival of Colours celebrates the end of winter with vibrant color throws and music, inspired by the Hindu spring festival.

1. **Hast du** Internet **auf deinem** Smartphone?
2. **Ja, ich habe** WLAN. **Ich benutze es für** soziale Medien **und** E-Mails.
3. **Hast du einen** Computer **oder** Laptop?
4. **Ich habe einen** Laptop. **Ich benutze ihn zum** Herunterladen von Dateien.
5. **Welchen** Browser benutzt du?
6. **Ich benutze die** App von Google Chrome.

❖ In German, the stress is usually on the first syllable of a word, making it important for pronunciation, especially in technology terms.

1. **Do you have** Internet **on your** Smartphone?
2. **Yes, I have** Wi-Fi. **I use it for** social media **and** emails.
3. **Do you have a** Computer **or** Laptop?
4. **I have a** Laptop. **I use it for** downloading files.
5. **Which** Browser do you use?
6. **I use the** App from Google Chrome.

✤ In 1609, Germany launched the world's first weekly newspaper, laying the foundation for modern journalism.

1. Guten Morgen! Wo ist die **Fernbedienung** für den **Fernseher**?
2. Sie liegt auf dem Tisch. Welchen **Kanal** möchtest du sehen?
3. Ich möchte die **Nachrichten** sehen. Kannst du den **Drucker** einschalten?
4. Ja, das kann ich. Brauchst du den **Monitor** oder die **Kamera**?
5. Nein, ich brauche nur den **Drucker**. Danke!

✤ In German, there are no written accents like in Spanish or French; every letter is pronounced without altering its sound due to accent marks.

1. Good morning! Where is the **remote control** for the **TV**?
2. It's on the table. Which **channel** would you like to watch?
3. I want to watch the **news**. Can you turn on the **printer**?
4. Yes, I can. Do you need the **monitor** or the **camera**?
5. No, I just need the **printer**. Thank you!

✤ In Germany, a social network for gardeners called "GartenNetzwerk" has become a vibrant community where members swap plants and share gardening tips.

CHALLENGE NO. 5

LISTEN TO A PODCAST IN GERMAN AND SUMMARIZE IT, IN WRITING OR ORALLY.

"Die Neugier ist der Schlüssel zur Erkenntnis."

"Curiosity is the key to knowledge."

1. Hallo Peter, was ist dein Lieblings**tier**?
2. Ich mag viele Tiere, aber mein Lieblings**tier** ist der **Hund**.
3. Warum magst du Hunde?
4. Sie sind treu und spielen gerne. Und dein Lieblings**tier**?
5. Ich liebe **Katzen**. Sie sind so süß und unabhängig.
6. Ja, Katzen sind auch toll. Hast du andere Lieblingstiere?
7. Ja, ich mag auch **Vögel** und **Fische**.
8. Das ist interessant. Ich mag auch **Pferde** und **Kühe**.

❖ In German, to say you have a pet, link "haben" with the animal, like "Ich habe einen Hund" for "I have a dog."

1. Hello Peter, what's your favorite **animal**?
2. I like many animals, but my favorite **animal** is the **dog**.
3. Why do you like dogs?
4. They are loyal and love to play. And your favorite **animal**?
5. I love **cats**. They are so cute and independent.
6. Yes, cats are great too. Do you have other favorite animals?
7. Yes, I also like **birds** and **fish**.
8. That's interesting. I also like **horses** and **cows**.

✤ The black eagle is a proud symbol of Germany, representing power and strength, and has been used in the country's coat of arms since the Holy Roman Empire.

1. Hallo Peter, magst du die **Natur**?
2. Ja, ich liebe die **Natur**. Besonders mag ich den **Wald** und den **Berg**.
3. Ich auch. Ich liebe die **Pflanzen** im **Wald**. Die **Bäume**, das **Gras** und die **Blumen** sind so schön.
4. Ja, und die **Blätter** im Herbst sind so bunt. Hast du einen Lieblings**baum**?
5. Ja, ich liebe die Eiche. Und du?
6. Ich mag die Kiefer. Sie ist so groß und stark.

❖ In German, when a noun ending in "-e" is followed by a word starting with a vowel, we often drop the "-e" for easier pronunciation, like in "im alten Garten" becoming "im altn Garten".

DAY 52: PLANTS AND NATURE

1. Hello Peter, do you like **nature**?
2. Yes, I love **nature**. I especially like the **forest** and the **mountain**.
3. Me too. I love the **plants** in the **forest**. The **trees**, the **grass**, and the **flowers** are so beautiful.
4. Yes, and the **leaves** in autumn are so colorful. Do you have a favorite **tree**?
5. Yes, I love the oak. And you?
6. I like the pine. It's so tall and strong.

✤ In Germany, chamomile is not just a tea but a traditional remedy used for centuries to soothe stomach aches and calm nerves.

1. Hallo Tom, wie viele **Blumen** hast du in deinem Garten?
2. Ich habe **einunddreißig** Rosen und **zweiunddreißig** Tulpen.
3. Und wie viele **Bäume** hast du?
4. Ich habe **dreiunddreißig** Apfelbäume und **vierunddreißig** Kirschbäume.
5. Wow, das ist viel! Und wie viele **Pflanzen** hast du im Haus?
6. Ich habe **fünfunddreißig** Zimmerpflanzen.
7. Das ist beeindruckend! Du musst sehr **erfreut** sein, so viel Grün um dich herum zu haben.
8. Ja, das bin ich. Es macht mich sehr glücklich.

✤ In German, when using numbers like "einunddreißig" (31), there's no space between parts; it's like saying "oneandthirty" all as one word.

1. Hello Tom, how many **flowers** do you have in your garden?
2. I have **thirty-one** roses and **thirty-two** tulips.
3. And how many **trees** do you have?
4. I have **thirty-three** apple trees and **thirty-four** cherry trees.
5. Wow, that's a lot! And how many **plants** do you have in the house?
6. I have **thirty-five** houseplants.
7. That's impressive! You must be very **pleased** to have so much greenery around you.
8. Yes, I am. It makes me very happy.

♣ Germany's Neuschwanstein Castle inspired Disneyland's Sleeping Beauty Castle and was constructed with 465 tons of Salzburg marble.

1. Hallo Peter, magst du **Musik**?

2. Ja, ich liebe Musik. Ich höre gerne **Radio** und gehe zu **Konzerten**.

3. Cool! Spielst du ein Instrument?

4. Nein, aber ich singe gerne. Ich bin in einer **Band**.

5. Das ist toll! Was ist dein Lieblings**lied**?

6. Mein Lieblingslied ist "Bohemian Rhapsody". Und du?

7. Ich liebe auch Musik, aber ich tanze lieber. Ich gehe oft ins **Theater** oder sehe einen **Film**.

8. Das klingt nach Spaß!

✤ In German, the determiner changes form based on the gender of the noun, so for "the song" we say "das Lied" because "Lied" is neutral.

1. Hello Peter, do you like **music**?
2. Yes, I love music. I enjoy listening to the **radio** and going to **concerts**.
3. Cool! Do you play an instrument?
4. No, but I like to sing. I'm in a **band**.
5. That's great! What's your favorite **song**?
6. My favorite song is "Bohemian Rhapsody". And you?
7. I also love music, but I prefer dancing. I often go to the **theater** or watch a **movie**.
8. That sounds like fun!

✤ In Germany, the Alphorn, originally a communication device in the Alps, is now celebrated in festivals and concerts.

1. **Hallo, wie komme ich zum** Flughafen?
2. **Sie können ein** Taxi **nehmen oder mit dem** Bus fahren.
3. **Und wenn ich zum** Bahnhof will?
4. **Sie können den** Zug **nehmen oder mit dem** Auto fahren.
5. **Und wie komme ich zum** Hafen?
6. **Sie können ein** Fahrrad mieten oder zu Fuß gehen.

✤ In German, to express "some" or "any" when talking about means of transportation, use "einige" for plural and "etwas" for uncountable nouns.

1. **Hello, how do I get to the** Airport?
2. **You can take a** Taxi **or go by** Bus.
3. **And if I want to go to the** Train Station?
4. **You can take the** Train **or go by** Car.
5. **And how do I get to the** Port?
6. **You can rent a** Bike or walk.

✤ In the 19th century, thousands of Germans migrated to Texas, forming a unique cultural enclave known as the Texas German Belt.

TAG NR. 56: SHOPPING II 🌱

1. Hallo Peter, willst du mit mir ins
   Einkaufszentrum gehen?
2. Ja, ich brauche neue **Kleidung**. Ich brauche eine
   neue **Jacke**.
3. Wir können auch ins **Lebensmittelgeschäft** gehen.
   Es ist im **Einkaufszentrum**.
4. Das ist eine gute Idee. Ich brauche auch neuen
   Schmuck. Eine **Halskette** und **Ohrringe**.
5. Perfekt! Es gibt einen **Verkauf** im
   Einkaufszentrum. Wir bekommen einen guten
   Rabatt.

✤ To show possession in German, add "-s" or "-es" to the end of a noun, like "Marias Buch"

(Maria's book).

1. Hello Peter, do you want to go to the **shopping mall** with me?
2. Yes, I need new **clothes**. I need a new **jacket**.
3. We can also go to the **grocery store**. It's in the **shopping mall**.
4. That's a good idea. I also need new **jewelry**. A **necklace** and **earrings**.
5. Perfect! There's a **sale** at the **shopping mall**. We'll get a good **discount**.

✤ In Germany, flea markets are often called "Flohmarkt," where one can find treasures from the past, making them a nostalgic journey through time.

1. Hallo Peter, wie geht es dir? Du siehst nicht gut aus.

2. Mein **Rücken** tut weh und ich habe Kopfschmerzen.

3. Hast du Fieber? Fühlst du deinen **Arm** oder dein **Bein**?

4. Nein, mein **Arm** und mein **Bein** sind in Ordnung. Aber mein **Kopf** tut sehr weh.

5. Vielleicht solltest du zum Arzt gehen. Er kann dein **Ohr**, dein **Auge**, deine **Nase**, deinen **Mund** und deine **Zähne** überprüfen.

✤ In German, to point out something related to body and health, use "dieser, diese, dieses" for "this" and "jener, jene, jenes" for "that," matching the gender and number of the noun they describe.

1. Hello Peter, how are you? You don't look well.
2. My **back** hurts and I have a headache.
3. Do you have a fever? Can you feel your **arm** or your **leg**?
4. No, my **arm** and my **leg** are fine. But my **head** hurts a lot.
5. Maybe you should go to the doctor. He can check your **ear**, your **eye**, your **nose**, your **mouth**, and your **teeth**.

✤ In Germany, the practice of using leeches for medicinal purposes, a method dating back to ancient times, is still utilized today in some modern clinics.

1. **Guten Morgen, Herr** Arzt. Was sind Sie von Beruf?

2. **Ich bin** Zahnarzt. Und Sie?

3. **Ich bin** Anwalt. **Mein Bruder ist** Lehrer **und meine Schwester ist** Kellnerin.

4. **Interessant. Mein Vater ist** Koch **und meine Mutter ist** Managerin.

5. **Mein Onkel ist** Präsident **einer Firma und meine Tante ist** Autorin.

6. **Und mein Cousin ist** Schauspieler. Er liebt seinen Beruf.

✤ In German, to describe a profession someone has, you use "sein" as the auxiliary verb, like "Er ist Arzt" (He is a doctor), and to add more about the job, use a relative clause starting with "der, die, das" depending on the gender of the profession, for example, "Er ist ein Arzt, der in einem Krankenhaus arbeitet" (He is a doctor who works in a hospital).

1. **Good morning, Mr.** Doctor. What is your profession?
2. **I am a** Dentist. And you?
3. **I am a** Lawyer. **My brother is a** Teacher **and my sister is a** Waitress.
4. **Interesting. My father is a** Chef **and my mother is a** Manager.
5. **My uncle is the** President **of a company and my aunt is an** Author.
6. **And my cousin is an** Actor. He loves his job.

✤ In Germany, the art of making cuckoo clocks, a tradition that started in the Black Forest region in the 18th century, is still meticulously preserved by skilled artisans.

1. **Guten Morgen! Wo ist das** Sofa?
2. **Das Sofa ist neben dem** Tisch **und dem** Stuhl.
3. **Und wo ist der** Kühlschrank?
4. **Der Kühlschrank ist neben dem** Ofen.
5. **Wo ist die** Lampe?
6. **Die Lampe ist über dem** Tisch.
7. **Wo ist das** Bett?
8. **Das Bett ist neben dem** Fenster **und der** Tür.
9. **Und wo ist die** Uhr?
10. **Die Uhr ist über der** Tür.

✤ In German, to talk about an indefinite amount of household items, use "ein" or "eine" before the noun, depending on the gender of the noun.

1. **Good morning! Where is the** Sofa?
2. **The sofa is next to the** Table **and the** Chair.
3. **And where is the** Refrigerator?
4. **The refrigerator is next to the** Oven.
5. **Where is the** Lamp?
6. **The lamp is above the** Table.
7. **Where is the** Bed?
8. **The bed is next to the** Window **and the** Door.
9. **And where is the** Clock?
10. **The clock is above the** Door.

❖ Germany invented the Christmas tree tradition in the 16th century, bringing evergreens into homes for decoration.

1. Hallo Peter, wie groß ist dein **Sofa**?
2. Die **Länge** ist zwei **Meter**, die **Breite** ist ein **Meter** und die **Höhe** ist ein halber **Meter**.
3. Und wie viel **Gewicht** hat es?
4. Es wiegt zwanzig **Kilogramm**.
5. Wow, das ist ziemlich groß und schwer. Wie groß ist dein **Fernseher**?
6. Der **Fernseher** ist 55 **Zoll**.
7. Das ist beeindruckend! Und wie groß ist dein **Kühlschrank**?
8. Der **Kühlschrank** ist 180 **Zentimeter** hoch.

❖ In German, to form the present participle of verbs related to measurements and size, add "end" to the stem, like "messend" for measuring.

1. Hello Peter, how big is your **sofa**?
2. The **length** is two **meters**, the **width** is one **meter**, and the **height** is half a **meter**.
3. And how much does it **weigh**?
4. It weighs twenty **kilograms**.
5. Wow, that's quite big and heavy. How big is your **TV**?
6. The **TV** is 55 **inches**.
7. That's impressive! And how big is your **refrigerator**?
8. The **refrigerator** is 180 **centimeters** tall.

✤ In ancient Germany, the length of a foot varied by region, leading to the saying, "Every town has its own foot."

CHALLENGE NO. 6

RECORD A SHORT AUDIO WHERE YOU TALK ABOUT YOUR PROGRESS IN GERMAN.

"Kulturelle Vielfalt bereichert unser Leben."

"Cultural diversity enriches our lives."

1. Hallo Tom, was möchtest du zum Abendessen?
2. Ich hätte gerne **Nudeln** mit **Butter** und **Pfeffer**.
3. Möchtest du dazu **Rindfleisch, Hähnchen oder Schweinefleisch?**
4. Ich nehme das **Hähnchen**. Und danach vielleicht ein Stück **Brot** mit **Käse**.
5. Sehr gut. Und zum Nachtisch? Vielleicht **Eiscreme oder Reispudding?**
6. Oh, **Eiscreme** klingt gut!

✤ In German, to form the past participle of regular verbs, add "ge-" at the beginning and "-t" at the end of the verb stem, as in "gekocht" for "to cook."

1. Hello Tom, what would you like for dinner?
2. I would like **pasta** with **butter** and **pepper**.
3. Would you like **beef, chicken, or pork** with that?
4. I'll have the **chicken**. And maybe a piece of **bread** with **cheese** afterwards.
5. Very good. And for dessert? Maybe **ice cream** or **rice pudding**?
6. Oh, **ice cream** sounds good!

✤ In Germany, the 19th-century introduction of the potato, initially met with skepticism, revolutionized the nation's cuisine and became a staple ingredient.

1. Guten Morgen, Peter. Wie war dein **Montag**?
2. Hallo Anna. Mein **Montag** war gut. Und dein **Dienstag**?
3. Mein **Dienstag** war auch gut. Was hast du am **Mittwoch** gemacht?
4. Am **Mittwoch** habe ich gearbeitet. Und du am **Donnerstag**?
5. Am **Donnerstag** habe ich mich mit Freunden getroffen. Freust du dich auf das **Wochenende**?
6. Ja, ich freue mich auf das **Wochenende**. Ich werde am **Samstag** und **Sonntag** entspannen.
7. Das klingt gut. Ich wünsche dir eine schöne **Woche**.

❖ In German, days of the week are capitalized and do not use the gerund form.

1. Good morning, Peter. How was your **Monday**?

2. Hello Anna. My **Monday** was good. And your **Tuesday**?

3. My **Tuesday** was also good. What did you do on **Wednesday**?

4. On **Wednesday**, I worked. And you on **Thursday**?

5. On **Thursday**, I met up with friends. Are you looking forward to the **weekend**?

6. Yes, I'm looking forward to the **weekend**. I will relax on **Saturday** and **Sunday**.

7. That sounds good. I wish you a nice **week**.

✤ In Germany, it's not uncommon for newspapers to have a dedicated section for horoscopes, reflecting the day's astrological forecast.

1. **Guten** Morgen! **Wie war dein** Tag gestern?
2. **Es war gut. Und dein** Abend?
3. **Er war ruhig. Was machst du** morgen?
4. **Ich werde im** Park **spazieren gehen. Es ist** Frühling, die perfekte Zeit dafür.
5. **Das klingt schön. Ich liebe den** Sommer mehr.
6. **Ich auch, aber der** Winter ist auch schön.
7. **Ja, jede** Jahreszeit hat ihre eigene Schönheit.

✤ In German, to talk about liking or disliking weather in a specific season, use "mögen" plus the infinitive of the weather verb, like "Ich mag es, im Sommer zu schwimmen" (I like to swim in the summer).

1. **Good** morning! How was your **day** yesterday?
2. **It was good. And your** evening?
3. **It was quiet. What are you doing** tomorrow?
4. **I will go for a walk in the** park. **It's** spring, the perfect time for it.
5. **That sounds nice. I love** summer more.
6. **Me too, but** winter is also beautiful.
7. **Yes, every** season has its own beauty.

✤ In Germany, the song "Der Mai ist gekommen" celebrates the joy and renewal brought by the month of May, marking the heart of spring.

1. Hallo **Tante** Maria, wie geht es dir?
2. Hallo Anna, mir geht es gut. Und wie geht es deinem **Onkel** Peter?
3. **Onkel** Peter geht es gut. Er spielt gerade mit meinem **Neffen** Max im Garten.
4. Das ist schön. Wie geht es deiner **Nichte** Lisa und deinem **Enkel** Tom?
5. Lisa und Tom sind bei meiner **Cousine** Julia. Sie haben heute einen schönen Tag.
6. Und dein **Verlobter** Paul? Ist er bei der Arbeit?
7. Ja, er ist mit seinem **Kollegen** Markus bei der Arbeit. Sie haben heute viel zu tun.

❖ In German, many family-related words share a common root, like "Bruder" (brother) and "Schwester" (sister), showing their connection.

1. Hello **Aunt** Maria, how are you?
2. Hello Anna, I'm doing well. And how is your **Uncle** Peter?
3. **Uncle** Peter is doing well. He's currently playing with my **nephew** Max in the garden.
4. That's nice. How are your **niece** Lisa and your **grandson** Tom?
5. Lisa and Tom are with my **cousin** Julia. They're having a nice day today.
6. And your **fiancé** Paul? Is he at work?
7. Yes, he's at work with his **colleague** Markus. They have a lot to do today.

✤ In Germany, it's common for families to pass down the recipe for "Eierlikör," a traditional homemade eggnog, as a cherished holiday tale.

1. Hallo Peter, wo ist der **Flughafen**?
2. Der Flughafen ist **weit** von hier. Du musst **links abbiegen und dann geradeaus** fahren.
3. Und wo ist das **Badezimmer**?
4. Das Badezimmer ist **oben**. Es ist **zwischen** dem **Bett** und dem **Sofa**.
5. Und wo kann ich **anhalten** um zu essen?
6. Es gibt ein Restaurant **nahe** hier. Es ist **rechts** von der **Bushaltestelle**.

✤ In German, when giving directions, remember to conjugate the verb to match the subject doing the action, like "gehen" becomes "ich gehe" for "I go".

1. Hello Peter, where is the **airport**?
2. The airport is **far** from here. You need to **turn left** and then go **straight**.
3. And where is the **bathroom**?
4. The bathroom is **upstairs**. It is **between** the **bed** and the **sofa**.
5. And where can I **stop** to eat?
6. There's a restaurant **near** here. It is **to the right** of the **bus stop**.

✤ Johann Wolfgang von Goethe's Italian Journey inspired a surge in German tourism to Italy, shaping the Grand Tour tradition.

1. Hallo Tom, du siehst **aufgeregt** aus. Was ist los?
2. Ich bin ein bisschen **nervös**. Ich habe morgen ein Vorstellungsgespräch.
3. Oh, das ist **aufregend**! Aber warum bist du **besorgt**?
4. Ich bin nicht sicher, ob ich gut genug bin.
5. Sei nicht **ängstlich**. Du solltest **stolz** auf dich sein. Du bist sehr qualifiziert.
6. Danke Anna, das macht mich **beruhigt**. Ich war nur ein bisschen **gestresst**.
7. Kein Problem, Tom. Es ist normal, sich ein bisschen **unsicher** zu fühlen. Du wirst großartig sein!

✤ In German, to express feelings in the past, we often use the compound tense "haben" or "sein" as auxiliary verbs with the past participle of the emotion verb.

1. Hello Tom, you look **excited**. What's up?
2. I'm a bit **nervous**. I have a job interview tomorrow.
3. Oh, that's **exciting**! But why are you **worried**?
4. I'm not sure if I'm good enough.
5. Don't be **anxious**. You should be **proud** of yourself. You're very qualified.
6. Thank you, Anna, that makes me **reassured**. I was just a bit **stressed**.
7. No problem, Tom. It's normal to feel a bit **uncertain**. You're going to be great!

✤ In Germany, the Sturm und Drang movement of the late 18th century celebrated intense emotion as an authentic source of aesthetic experience, profoundly influencing literature, music, and art.

1. **Hallo, kannst du mir helfen? Mein** Internet funktioniert nicht.
2. **Natürlich, hast du dein** WLAN überprüft?
3. **Ja, es funktioniert auf meinem** Smartphone, aber nicht auf meinem Laptop.
4. **Hast du versucht, eine** Webseite **in einem anderen** Browser zu öffnen?
5. Nein, ich werde das jetzt versuchen.
6. **Und vergiss nicht, deine** E-Mails **und** Soziale Medien auf deinem Smartphone zu überprüfen.
7. **Gute Idee! Ich werde auch die** Apps auf meinem Smartphone überprüfen.
8. Ja, das ist eine gute Idee. Viel Glück!

✤ In German, to express wanting to do something related to technology and media, use the infinitive form of the verb with "möchten," like "Ich möchte ein Foto machen" (I want to take a photo).

1. **Hello, can you help me? My** Internet is not working.
2. **Of course, have you checked your** Wi-Fi?
3. **Yes, it works on my** Smartphone, but not on my laptop.
4. **Have you tried opening a** website **in a different** browser?
5. No, I will try that now.
6. **And don't forget to check your** Emails **and** Social Media on your smartphone.
7. **Good idea! I will also check the** Apps on my smartphone.
8. Yes, that's a good idea. Good luck!

✤ In 1609, Germany launched the world's first weekly newspaper, laying the foundation for modern journalism.

1. Hallo Peter, was machst du gerade?
2. Ich **lese** ein **Buch**. Es ist ein interessanter **Roman**.
3. Oh, ich dachte, du magst **Poesie** mehr als **Fiktion**.
4. Das ist richtig. Aber manchmal lese ich auch **Sachbücher**.
5. Und was ist mit Kunst? Magst du **Fotografie**, **Zeichnung oder Malerei**?
6. Ich mag alle drei, aber ich liebe es besonders, zu **singen**.

✤ In German, the participle mode is often used to describe actions related to reading and arts, like "lesend" (reading) or "malend" (painting), to show someone is doing these activities.

1. Hello Peter, what are you doing right now?
2. I **am reading** a **book. It's an interesting novel**.
3. Oh, I thought you liked **poetry** more than **fiction**.
4. That's true. But sometimes I also read **non-fiction**.
5. And what about art? Do you like **photography, drawing, or painting**?
6. I like all three, but I especially love to **sing**.

❖ The Neues Museum in Berlin was meticulously reconstructed with its original 19th-century details after being heavily damaged in World War II.

1. Hallo Tom, wo ist der **Flughafen**?
2. Der Flughafen ist neben dem **Bahnhof**. Du kannst ein **Taxi** nehmen.
3. Danke. Ich habe ein **Hotel** gebucht, aber ich finde auch eine **Herberge** oder ein **Gasthaus** gut.
4. Vergiss nicht, deine **Botschaft** zu informieren.
5. Ja, ich habe mein **Gepäck**, meinen **Rucksack** und meinen **Koffer** schon gepackt.

✤ In German, to express activities like traveling, we often use the gerund mode by adding "-ing" to the verb in English, but in German, we use the infinitive form with "zu" like "zu reisen" for "traveling."

1. Hello Tom, where is the **airport**?
2. The airport is next to the **train station**. You can take a **taxi**.
3. Thank you. I have booked a **hotel**, but I also like a **hostel** or an **inn**.
4. Don't forget to inform your **embassy**.
5. Yes, I have already packed my **luggage**, my **backpack**, and my **suitcase**.

✤ In Germany, the Cologne Cathedral, a masterpiece of Gothic architecture, took over 600 years to complete.

1. Hallo, ich brauche ein **Taxi** zum **Bahnhof**. Wie viel kostet das?
2. Das kostet **sechzehn** Euro.
3. Okay, und wie lange dauert die Fahrt?
4. Ungefähr **fünfzehn** Minuten.
5. Gut, ich habe nur **zwanzig** Euro. Ist das in Ordnung?
6. Ja, das ist in Ordnung. Ich habe Wechselgeld.
7. Perfekt! Dann fahren wir los.

✤ In German, numbers 11-20 are used as adjectives and don't change form based on gender, case, or number.

1. Hello, I need a **taxi** to the **train station**. How much does that cost?
2. It costs **sixteen** euros.
3. Okay, and how long does the trip take?
4. About **fifteen** minutes.
5. Good, I only have **twenty** euros. Is that okay?
6. Yes, that's fine. I have change.
7. Perfect! Then let's go.

♣ In the iconic painting "The Last Supper" by Leonardo da Vinci, the arrangement of the apostles in groups of three and the use of triangles are believed to reflect the artist's interest in numerology and its symbolic significance.

CHALLENGE NO. 7

ENGAGE IN A 15-MINUTE CONVERSATION IN GERMAN ON EVERYDAY TOPICS.

"Gut Ding will Weile haben."

"Good things take time."

1. Wie alt bist du?
2. **Ich bin** einundzwanzig Jahre alt. Und du?
3. **Ich bin** vierundzwanzig. Hast du Geschwister?
4. **Ja, ich habe einen Bruder. Er ist** dreißig.
5. Und wie alt ist deine Schwester?
6. **Sie ist** siebenundzwanzig Jahre alt.

✤ In German, when using numbers from 21 to 30 in sentences, the verb agrees with the subject's number, not with the numeral itself.

1. How old are you?
2. **I am** twenty-one years old. And you?
3. **I am** twenty-four. Do you have any siblings?
4. **Yes, I have a brother. He is** thirty.
5. And how old is your sister?
6. **She is** twenty-seven years old.

✤ In Germany, the TV show "Raumpatrouille – Die phantastischen Abenteuer des Raum-schiffes Orion" became a cult classic, intriguing viewers in the 1960s with its imaginative use of mathematical concepts in space exploration.

1. Guten Tag! Wo ist das **Museum**?
2. Hallo! Es ist neben dem **Kalender-Festival**.
3. Ah, das **Festival** mit der **Tradition** und **Geschichte**?
4. Ja, genau. Es ist ein Teil unserer **Kultur**.
5. Interessant! Und wann ist der **Zeitplan** für das Festival?
6. Es beginnt am **Montag**.
7. Vielen Dank! Ich freue mich darauf.
8. Gern geschehen. Genießen Sie Ihren Aufenthalt!
9. Ich werde es sicher tun. Danke!

✤ Valency in German grammar refers to the number of arguments a verb requires to form a complete sentence.

1. Good day! Where is the **Museum**?
2. Hello! It's next to the **Calendar Festival**.
3. Ah, the **Festival** with the **Tradition** and **History**?
4. Yes, exactly. It's a part of our **Culture**.
5. Interesting! And what's the **Schedule** for the festival?
6. It starts on **Monday**.
7. Thank you! I'm looking forward to it.
8. You're welcome. Enjoy your stay!
9. I surely will. Thank you!

✤ In Germany, there's a tradition called "Kaffee und Kuchen," where people enjoy coffee and cake together in the afternoon, similar to British tea time.

1. Guten Morgen, Tom. Was machst du in der Küche?
2. Ich koche Frühstück. Kannst du mir den **Teller**, die **Gabel**, den **Löffel** und das **Messer** geben?
3. Natürlich. Brauchst du auch die **Pfanne** oder den **Topf**?
4. Nein, ich brauche nur den **Toaster**. Die Eier sind im **Kühlschrank** und das Brot ist im **Gefrierschrank**.
5. Alles klar. Und der **Ofen**? Brauchst du den auch?
6. Nein, danke. Nur der **Toaster** ist genug.

✤ In German, verbs related to cooking can be transitive (needing a direct object, like "Ich schneide das Gemüse" - I cut the vegetables) or intransitive (not needing a direct object, like "Das Wasser kocht" - The water boils).

DAY 73: COOKING AND KITCHEN II 🌱

1. Good morning, Tom. What are you doing in the kitchen?
2. I'm making breakfast. Can you pass me the **plate**, the **fork**, the **spoon**, and the **knife**?
3. Of course. Do you also need the **pan** or the **pot**?
4. No, I just need the **toaster**. The eggs are in the **fridge** and the bread is in the **freezer**.
5. All right. And the **oven**? Do you need that too?
6. No, thank you. Just the **toaster** is enough.

❖ Germany's "Das Perfekte Dinner" has turned ordinary home cooks into nationwide celebrities, showcasing the diversity of regional German cuisine.

1. **Guten Morgen, ich habe** Fieber **und** Husten.
2. **Oh nein, hast du auch** Kopfschmerzen?
3. **Ja, und auch** Zahnschmerzen.
4. **Vielleicht hast du eine** Allergie. **Du solltest eine** Pille **nehmen und viel** Flüssigkeit trinken.
5. **Ich habe kein** Rezept.
6. **Dann geh zur** Apotheke **oder zur** Klinik. Sie können dir helfen.

✤ In German, verbs related to feeling or being, like "sich fühlen" (to feel) or "krank sein" (to be sick), often don't take a direct object, showing intransitivity.

1. **Good morning, I have a** fever **and** cough.
2. **Oh no, do you also have** headaches?
3. **Yes, and also** toothache.
4. **Maybe you have an** allergy. **You should take a** pill **and drink lots of** fluids.
5. **I don't have a** prescription.
6. **Then go to the** pharmacy **or the** clinic. They can help you.

✤ In Germany, Robert Koch, a founding father of bacteriology, won the Nobel Prize in 1905 for his groundbreaking work on tuberculosis, significantly advancing public health.

1. Guten Morgen, **Lehrer**. Ich habe meine
   Hausaufgaben nicht gemacht.
2. Warum nicht?
3. Ich hatte eine **Prüfung** an der **Universität** und
   keine Zeit.
4. Du musst deine Zeit besser planen. Die **Schule** ist
   auch wichtig.
5. Ja, Sie haben recht. Ich werde in der nächsten
   Unterrichtsstunde besser sein.
6. Gut. Vergiss nicht, dein **Buch** und deinen **Stift**
   mitzubringen.
7. Natürlich, danke.

❖ In German, to express actions done to oneself, we add "-sich" before the verb, as in "Ich
wasche mich" (I wash myself).

1. Good morning, **teacher**. I didn't do my **homework**.
2. Why not?
3. I had an **exam** at the **university** and no time.
4. You need to plan your time better. **School** is important too.
5. Yes, you're right. I'll be better in the next **class**.
6. Good. Don't forget to bring your **book** and your **pen**.
7. Of course, thank you.

✤ Germany's dual education system combines apprenticeships in a company and vocational education at a vocational school in one course.

1. **Entschuldigung, wo ist der nächste** Geldautomat?
2. **Der** Geldautomat **ist um die Ecke. Brauchen Sie** Bargeld?
3. **Ja, ich habe nur meine** Kreditkarte dabei.
4. **Verstehe. Und denken Sie daran, Ihre** Quittung zu behalten.
5. **Natürlich. Wie ist der** Wechselkurs hier?
6. **Er ist nicht so** teuer. **Aber der** Preis kann variieren.
7. **Ich hoffe, ich brauche keine** Rückerstattung.
8. **Das hoffe ich auch. Gutes** Shopping!

✤ In German, to express reciprocity, especially when talking about transactions in shopping, we often use the reflexive pronoun "sich" with verbs, like "Sie kaufen sich ein Auto" (They buy themselves a car).

1. **Excuse me, where is the nearest** ATM?
2. **The** ATM is around the corner. Do you need **cash**?
3. Yes, I only have my **credit card** with me.
4. **I see. And remember to keep your** receipt.
5. **Of course. What's the** exchange rate here?
6. **It's not too** expensive. **But the** price can vary.
7. **I hope I don't need a** refund.
8. **I hope so too. Happy** shopping!

✤ In Germany, the board game "Monopoly" was adapted into "D-Mark Monopoly" after World War II, reflecting the country's economic recovery and the introduction of the Deutsche Mark.

1. Hallo, ich möchte im **Restaurant** essen.
2. Natürlich, hier ist die **Speisekarte**.
3. Ich nehme die **Vorspeise** Salat, das **Hauptgericht** Sandwich und als **Nachspeise** Schokolade.
4. Möchten Sie auch **Toast** mit **Marmelade**?
5. Ja, bitte.

✤ In German, to say who is doing the action in a sentence, we add 'von' plus the doer after the verb, like in "Das Essen wurde von dem Koch gemacht" (The meal was made by the cook).

DAY 77: EATING OUT II 🌱

1. Hello, I would like to eat at the **restaurant**.
2. Of course, here is the **menu**.
3. I'll have the **appetizer** salad, the **main course** sandwich, and for **dessert** chocolate.
4. Would you also like **toast** with **jam**?
5. Yes, please.

✤ In Germany, the Dresden Frauenkirche, destroyed during WWII, was meticulously restored using its original stones, reviving a centuries-old tradition of craftsmanship and community spirit.

1. **Guten Morgen! Ist das dein** Haus?
2. Ja, das ist mein Haus. Komm rein!
3. **Wow, dein** Sofa **ist sehr bequem. Und der** Tisch ist sehr groß.
4. **Danke! Das ist mein** Stuhl **und das ist mein** Bett.
5. **Dein** Fenster **ist sehr hell. Und wo ist die** Tür zum Badezimmer?
6. **Die Tür ist dort. Und das ist mein** Ofen **und mein** Kühlschrank.
7. Und was ist das?
8. **Das ist meine** Lampe. **Und das ist mein** Fernseher.

✤ In German, to describe using an object for a purpose, we often use the preposition "mit" (with) followed by the dative case.

1. **Good morning! Is this your** house?
2. Yes, this is my house. Come in!
3. **Wow, your** sofa **is very comfortable. And the** table is very big.
4. **Thank you! This is my** chair **and this is my** bed.
5. **Your** window **is very bright. And where is the** door to the bathroom?
6. **The door is over there. And this is my** oven **and my** refrigerator.
7. And what is this?
8. **This is my** lamp. **And this is my** television.

✤ In 19th century Germany, the Biedermeier period emphasized simple and practical interior design, reflecting a desire for comfort and a retreat from political unrest.

1. **Guten Morgen! Wie ist die** Vorhersage **für das** Wetter heute?
2. **Es wird** nass. **Es gibt einen** Sturm **mit** Donner **und** Blitz.
3. **Oh nein! Gibt es auch einen** Hurrikan **oder** Tornado?
4. **Nein, aber es gibt ein** Erdbeben **in der Nähe des** Vulkans.
5. Das ist beängstigend! Ich bleibe zu Hause.

✤ In German, to describe the weather, you often use an adverbial phrase, like "Es regnet stark" (It is raining heavily), where "stark" is the adverbial phrase describing how it is raining.

1. **Good morning! What's the** forecast **for the** weather today?
2. **It's going to be** wet. There's a **storm** with **thunder** and **lightning**.
3. Oh no! Is there also a **hurricane** or **tornado**?
4. No, but there is an **earthquake** near the **volcano**.
5. That's scary! I'm staying home.

✤ In Germany, it's believed that if cows are lying down, rain is on its way.

1. Hallo Peter, was machst du in deiner **Freizeit**?
2. Hallo Anna, ich gehe gerne **wandern** und **schwimmen**. Und du?
3. Ich liebe es, ins **Kino** zu gehen und **Theaterstücke** zu sehen. Manchmal gehe ich auch **tanzen**.
4. Das klingt toll! Im Winter gehe ich gerne **skifahren** und **snowboarden**.
5. Ich spiele auch gerne **Musik** und singe **Lieder**.
6. Das ist interessant! Vielleicht können wir eines Tages zusammen etwas machen.

✤ In German, to talk about when you do a hobby, place the time complement at the beginning or end of the sentence, like "Am Montag spiele ich Fußball" or "Ich spiele Fußball am Montag."

206

DAY 80: LEISURE AND HOBBIES II 🌱

1. Hello Peter, what do you do in your **free time**?
2. Hello Anna, I like to go **hiking** and **swimming**. And you?
3. I love going to the **movies** and watching **plays**. Sometimes I also go **dancing**.
4. That sounds great! In the winter, I like to go **skiing** and **snowboarding**.
5. I also like to play **music** and sing **songs**.
6. That's interesting! Maybe we can do something together one day.

✤ Albert Einstein, a German-born theoretical physicist, was an avid sailor, despite famously not being very good at it.

CHALLENGE NO. 8

SPEAK ONLY IN GERMAN FOR AN HOUR.

"Sprachen öffnen Türen zur Welt."

"Languages open doors to the world."

1. **Welches** Transportmittel **benutzt du am liebsten,** Zug, **Bus** oder **Auto?**
2. Ich fahre am liebsten mit dem **Zug**. Und du?
3. **Ich nehme meistens das Auto. Aber manchmal fahre ich auch mit dem** Fahrrad.
4. **Hast du schon mal mit einem** Flugzeug **oder** Schiff gereist?
5. **Ja, ich bin schon mit einem** Flugzeug **geflogen. Aber mit einem** Schiff bin ich noch nie gefahren.
6. **Und wie ist es mit der** U-Bahn **oder der** Straßenbahn?
7. **Ich fahre oft mit der** U-Bahn, **aber selten mit der** Straßenbahn.

✤ In German, to describe where something happens, place the adverbial of place after the verb, like in "Wir fahren morgen nach Berlin."

1. **Which** mode of transportation **do you prefer,** train, bus, or **car?**
2. I prefer traveling by **train**. How about you?
3. **I mostly use the car. But sometimes I also ride a** bicycle.
4. **Have you ever traveled by** plane **or** ship?
5. **Yes, I've flown on a** plane **before. But I've never traveled by** ship.
6. **What about the** subway **or** tram?
7. **I often use the** subway, **but rarely the** tram.

✤ In the 1880s, Karl Benz invented the first automobile in Germany, revolutionizing transportation worldwide.

1. **Guten Morgen! Ich plane eine Reise. Ich möchte einen** Berg **besteigen und einen** Fluss überqueren.

2. **Das klingt nach einem Abenteuer! Möchtest du auch den** Ozean sehen?

3. **Ja, und ich möchte auch einen** See besuchen. Aber ich möchte keine **Wüste** oder **Dschungel** besuchen.

4. **Verstehe. Wie wäre es mit einem** Wald **oder einem** Strand?

5. **Ein** Strand **wäre schön. Und vielleicht ein schönes** Tal oder eine **Insel**.

6. Das klingt nach einer tollen Reise!

✤ In German, to express a cause, use "wegen" followed by a noun in the genitive case, like in "wegen des Wetters" (because of the weather).

1. **Good morning! I'm planning a trip. I want to climb a** mountain **and cross a** river.
2. **That sounds like an adventure! Would you also like to see the** ocean?
3. **Yes, and I also want to visit a** lake. **But I don't want to visit a** desert **or** jungle.
4. **I see. How about a** forest **or a** beach?
5. **A beach would be nice. And maybe a beautiful** valley **or an** island.
6. That sounds like a great trip!

❖ Germany's first national park, the Bavarian Forest National Park, was established in 1970, marking a pivotal moment in the country's commitment to preserving its natural heritage.

1. **Guten** Morgen! **Was hast du** gestern gemacht?
2. **Ich bin am** Nachmittag gewandert. Und du?
3. **Ich habe am** Abend **ein Theaterstück gesehen. Was machst du** heute?
4. **Ich gehe** jetzt schwimmen. Und morgen?
5. Morgen **gehe ich Skifahren. Gute** Nacht!

❖ To express purpose in German, use "um... zu" before the infinitive verb at the end of the sentence.

DAY 83: TIME AND ROUTINE 🌱

1. **Good** Morning! **What did you do** yesterday?
2. **I went hiking in the** afternoon. And you?
3. **I saw a play in the** evening. **What are you doing** today?
4. **I'm going swimming** now. And tomorrow?
5. Tomorrow **I'm going skiing. Good** Night!

❧ In Germany, it's common to start the day with a hearty breakfast including various breads, cheeses, and cold cuts, known as "Frühstück."

TAG NR. 84: EMOTIONEN III 🌱

1. Hallo Tom, wie geht es dir heute?
2. Ich fühle mich ein bisschen **einsam** und **besorgt**. Und du?
3. Oh, das tut mir leid zu hören. Ich bin eigentlich ziemlich **erfreut** und **entspannt**.
4. Das ist schön. Ich bin auch ein bisschen **nervös** wegen meiner Allergie.
5. Hast du deine **Pille** genommen?
6. Ja, aber ich bin immer noch **verärgert** und **wütend**.
7. Versuche dich zu entspannen, Tom. Morgen wird ein besserer Tag sein.

✤ In German, to describe someone or something with more detail, we use a relative clause, which starts with words like "der, die, das" (who, which, that) depending on the gender and number of the noun it refers to.

1. Hello Tom, how are you today?
2. I feel a bit **lonely** and **worried**. And you?
3. Oh, I'm sorry to hear that. I'm actually quite **pleased** and **relaxed**.
4. That's nice. I'm also a bit **nervous** about my allergy.
5. Did you take your **pill**?
6. Yes, but I'm still **upset** and **angry**.
7. Try to relax, Tom. Tomorrow will be a better day.

✤ In Germany, the Oktoberfest is not just a beer festival but a celebration of camaraderie and joy, drawing millions into an emotional collective.

TAG 85: FARBEN UND FORMEN 🌱

1. Hallo Tom, was ist deine Lieblingsfarbe?
2. Meine Lieblingsfarbe ist **Blau**. Und deine?
3. Ich mag **Rot**. Hast du eine Lieblingsform?
4. Ja, ich mag **runde** Formen. Und du?
5. Ich bevorzuge **quadratische** Formen. Sie sind sehr interessant.
6. Ja, das stimmt. Jeder hat seine eigenen Vorlieben.

✤ In German, when describing colors and shapes together, use "und" to connect them, like "rot und rund" for "red and round."

DAY 85: COLORS AND SHAPES 🌱

1. Hello Tom, what's your favorite color?
2. My favorite color is **Blue**. And yours?
3. I like **Red**. Do you have a favorite shape?
4. Yes, I like **round** shapes. And you?
5. I prefer **square** shapes. They are very interesting.
6. Yes, that's true. Everyone has their own preferences.

❖ In German Bauhaus art, the circle often symbolizes unity and harmony, reflecting the school's emphasis on total art integration.

1. Hallo, **Kollegin**! Wie geht es deiner **Familie**?
2. Hallo, **Anna**! Meiner **Familie** geht es gut, danke. Und deinem **Freund**?
3. Mein **Freund** ist jetzt mein **Verlobter**!
4. Oh, herzlichen Glückwunsch! Und wie geht es deinem **Nachbar**?
5. Mein **Nachbar**, der auch mein **Cousin** ist, geht es gut.
6. Und dein **Ehemann**?
7. Ich habe keinen **Ehemann**, ich bin verlobt!
8. Ach so, Entschuldigung. Ich habe es vergessen.
9. Kein Problem, **Lisa**. Das passiert.

❖ In German, to express relationships in time, cause, or condition, we use adverbial clauses introduced by conjunctions like "weil" (because), "wenn" (if/when), or "als" (when for past events).

DAY 86: RELATIONSHIPS ✎

1. Hello, **colleague**! How is your **family**?
2. Hello, **Anna**! My **family** is doing well, thank you. And your **boyfriend**?
3. My **boyfriend** is now my **fiancé**!
4. Oh, congratulations! And how is your **neighbor**?
5. My **neighbor**, who is also my **cousin**, is doing well.
6. And your **husband**?
7. I don't have a **husband**, I'm engaged!
8. Oh, sorry. I forgot.
9. No problem, **Lisa**. It happens.

❖ In Germany, the classic novel "The Sorrows of Young Werther" by Goethe sparked a fashion trend among young men who emulated Werther's clothing, showcasing the profound impact of literature on love, friendship, and even fashion in German culture.

1. Hallo Peter, ich mag deine **Kleidung**. Ist das eine neue **Jacke**?

2. Ja, und ich habe auch neue **Schuhe**. Magst du meinen **Hut**?

3. Ja, und die **Sonnenbrille** passt gut dazu.

4. Danke. Dein **Hemd** und deine **Hose** sehen auch toll aus. Ist das ein neuer **Rock**?

5. Ja, und ich trage auch eine neue **Halskette** und **Ohrringe**.

6. Sehr schön, Anna. Du siehst immer gut aus.

❖ In German, to compare two items of clothing, use "als" after the adjective, like "Mein Hemd ist größer als deine Hose." (My shirt is bigger than your pants.)

1. Hello Peter, I like your **clothes**. Is that a new **jacket**?
2. Yes, and I also have new **shoes**. Do you like my **hat**?
3. Yes, and the **sunglasses** go well with it.
4. Thank you. Your **shirt** and **pants** also look great. Is that a new **skirt**?
5. Yes, and I'm also wearing a new **necklace** and **earrings**.
6. Very nice, Anna. You always look good.

✤ In the 16th century, German men popularized the codpiece, a fashion statement that emphasized masculinity in an extravagant manner.

1. Hallo Tom, schaust du die **Nachrichten** auf dem **Fernseher**?
2. Nein, ich höre sie auf dem **Radio**. Wo ist die **Fernbedienung**?
3. Sie liegt neben dem **Computer**. Hast du dein **Smartphone** gesehen?
4. Ja, es ist in meiner Tasche. Ich muss eine **E-Mail** senden.
5. Vergiss nicht, auf den **sozialen Medien** zu posten.
6. Ja, ich werde es online tun.

❖ In German, to express a reason or cause, we use "weil" or "da" at the beginning of a causal clause, which sends the conjugated verb to the end of the clause.

1. Hello Tom, are you watching the **news** on the **television**?
2. No, I listen to it on the **radio**. Where is the **remote control**?
3. It's next to the **computer**. Have you seen your **smartphone**?
4. Yes, it's in my bag. I need to send an **email**.
5. Don't forget to post on **social media**.
6. Yes, I will do it online.

❖ Germany hosted the world's first cinema, opened by the Skladanowsky brothers in Berlin, 1895, showcasing the power of film technology.

1. **Was möchtest du zum Abendessen,** Fleisch **oder**
   Gemüse?
2. **Ich möchte** Gemüse **und etwas** Obst danach.
3. **Und was möchtest du trinken?** Wasser, Saft, Bier,
   Tee, Kaffee **oder** Milch?
4. **Ich nehme eine** Limonade, bitte.
5. **Ok, eine** Limonade. Und zum Nachtisch?
6. Ich nehme einen Apfel.

❖ If you were hungry, you would order food.

1. **What would you like for dinner,** Meat **or** Vegetables?
2. **I would like** Vegetables **and some** Fruit afterwards.
3. **And what would you like to drink?** Water, Juice, Beer, Tea, Coffee, **or** Milk?
4. **I'll have a** Lemonade, please.
5. **Ok, one** Lemonade. And for dessert?
6. I'll have an apple.

✤ In Germany, currywurst, a steamed then fried pork sausage cut into slices and seasoned with curry ketchup, is so beloved it has its own museum in Berlin.

1. Hallo Peter, wie ist dein **Haus**?
2. Hallo Anna, mein **Haus** ist groß. Es hat ein **Schlafzimmer**, ein **Badezimmer**, eine **Küche** und ein **Wohnzimmer**.
3. Hast du einen **Garten** oder einen **Hof**?
4. Ja, ich habe einen kleinen **Garten** und einen **Hof**. Es gibt auch eine **Garage** und einen **Balkon**.
5. Das klingt toll. Ich habe nur eine **Wohnung**.
6. Eine **Wohnung** ist auch schön, Anna.

✤ When talking about events in the past, present, or future at home, use a temporal clause starting with "als" for a single event in the past, "wenn" for repeated past events or future events, and "während" to describe something happening during another action.

1. Hello Peter, how is your **house**?
2. Hello Anna, my **house** is big. It has a **bedroom**, a **bathroom**, a **kitchen**, and a **living room**.
3. Do you have a **garden** or a **yard**?
4. Yes, I have a small **garden** and a **yard**. There's also a **garage** and a **balcony**.
5. That sounds great. I only have an **apartment**.
6. An **apartment** is also nice, Anna.

❖ Many historic German houses have "Stolpersteine" in front, small brass plaques commemorating the lives of those who were persecuted by the Nazis.

CHALLENGE NO. 9

WATCH A MOVIE IN GERMAN WITHOUT ENGLISH SUBTITLES AND SUMMARIZE THE STORY.

"Jeder kleine Erfolg ist es wert, gefeiert zu werden."

"Every small success is worth celebrating."

1. Hallo Peter, wohin gehst du?
2. Ich gehe zum **Supermarkt**. Ich brauche ein paar Sachen.
3. Hast du einen **Einkaufswagen** oder einen **Korb**?
4. Ich habe einen **Einkaufswagen**. Er ist einfacher zu schieben.
5. Ja, das stimmt. Vergiss nicht, die **Quittung** zu nehmen.
6. Ja, das werde ich. Vielleicht gibt es einen **Rabatt** oder einen **Verkauf**.
7. Das wäre toll. Pass auf den **Preis** auf.
8. Ja, das werde ich. Danke, Anna.

❖ In German, to express location, we use "wo" for "where" and "wohin" for "to where" in sentences about shopping and stores.

1. Hello Peter, where are you going?
2. I'm going to the **supermarket**. I need a few things.
3. Do you have a **shopping cart** or a **basket**?
4. I have a **shopping cart**. It's easier to push.
5. Yes, that's true. Don't forget to take the **receipt**.
6. Yes, I will. Maybe there's a **discount** or a **sale**.
7. That would be great. Watch out for the **price**.
8. Yes, I will. Thanks, Anna.

✤ In medieval Germany, guilds controlled retail trade, ensuring quality but also keeping prices high and competition low.

1. Hallo, **Polizei**? Ich brauche **Hilfe**. Es gibt einen **Notfall**.

2. Was ist passiert?

3. Es gibt ein **Feuer** in meinem Haus!

4. Bleiben Sie **sicher**, Anna. Der **Krankenwagen** und die Feuerwehr sind unterwegs.

5. Ich brauche auch einen **Arzt**. Mein Bruder hat sich verletzt.

6. Keine Sorge, Anna. Ein **Arzt** wird auch zum **Einsatzort** geschickt. Bleiben Sie weg von der **Gefahr**.

7. Danke, Polizei. Ich werde auf die **Erste Hilfe** warten.

✤ To express a purpose in German, use "um... zu" before the infinitive verb, as in "Ich lerne Deutsch, um im Notfall helfen zu können."

1. Hello, **Police**? I need **help**. There's an **emergency**.
2. What happened?
3. There's a **fire** in my house!
4. Stay **safe**, Anna. The **ambulance** and the fire department are on their way.
5. I also need a **doctor**. My brother is injured.
6. Don't worry, Anna. A **doctor** will also be sent to the **scene**. Stay away from the **danger**.
7. Thank you, police. I'll wait for the **first aid**.

✤ In WWII, German officer Wilm Hosenfeld heroically saved Polish pianist Władysław Szpilman, inspiring the film "The Pianist."

1. Entschuldigung, wo ist der **Flughafen**?
2. Der Flughafen ist in der Nähe. Haben Sie Ihr
   Ticket und **Reisepass**?
3. Ja, und ich habe auch eine **Reservierung** im **Hotel**.
4. Sehr gut. Und Ihr **Gepäck**?
5. Ich habe einen **Rucksack** und einen **Koffer**.
6. Perfekt. Hier ist eine **Karte** vom Flughafen.
7. Danke für Ihre Hilfe!

✤ Even though it's raining, we can still visit the museum.

1. Excuse me, where is the **airport**?
2. The airport is nearby. Do you have your **ticket** and **passport**?
3. Yes, and I also have a **reservation** at a **hotel**.
4. Very good. And your **luggage**?
5. I have a **backpack** and a **suitcase**.
6. Perfect. Here is a **map** of the airport.
7. Thank you for your help!

✤ The Hotel Adlon in Berlin, famously known for its luxurious hospitality, once hosted an elephant in a guest room as part of a circus promotion.

1. Hallo Peter, hast du Haustiere?
2. Ja, ich habe einen **Hund** und eine **Katze**. Und du?
3. Ich habe einen **Vogel** und einen **Fisch**. Meine Schwester hat ein **Pferd**.
4. Wow, ein Pferd! Mein Onkel hat eine **Kuh**, ein **Schaf**, eine **Ziege**, ein **Huhn** und ein **Schwein** auf seinem Bauernhof.
5. Das sind viele Tiere!

✤ In German, to add an explanatory clause about animals or pets, use "das ist" or "das sind" followed by the explanation, like in "Das ist mein Hund, der sehr schnell läuft." (That's my dog, who runs very fast.)

1. Hello Peter, do you have any pets?
2. Yes, I have a **dog** and a **cat**. And you?
3. I have a **bird** and a **fish**. My sister has a **horse**.
4. Wow, a horse! My uncle has a **cow**, a **sheep**, a **goat**, a **chicken**, and a **pig** on his farm.
5. That's a lot of animals!

✤ A bear named Wojtek joined the Polish army during WWII, carrying ammunition and boosting morale.

1. Guten Morgen, **Chef**. Ich habe den **Bericht** für die **Besprechung** fertig.
2. Sehr gut. Ist die **Präsentation** für die **Konferenz** auch fertig?
3. Ja, sie ist fertig. Aber ich habe eine Frage zur **Frist**.
4. Was ist deine Frage?
5. Ist die **Frist** für den nächsten **Bericht** am Freitag?
6. Ja, das ist richtig. Und bitte, sprich mit deinem **Kollegen** im **Büro** darüber.

✤ In direct speech, we use quotation marks to show someone's exact words, like "Ich bin Arzt," sagte er.

1. Good morning, **Boss**. I have finished the **report** for the **meeting**.
2. Very good. Is the **presentation** for the **conference** also ready?
3. Yes, it's ready. But I have a question about the **deadline**.
4. What's your question?
5. Is the **deadline** for the next **report** on Friday?
6. Yes, that's correct. And please, talk to your **colleague** in the **office** about it.

✤ Albert Einstein, a German-born physicist, revolutionized our understanding of the universe by introducing the theory of relativity.

1. Guten Morgen, Kollege. Welcher Tag ist heute?
2. Heute ist **Montag**.
3. Und welcher Monat ist es?
4. Es ist **Januar**.
5. Danke. Ich muss meinen **Kalender** aktualisieren.
6. Kein Problem. Hast du Pläne für das Wochenende?
7. Ja, ich habe eine **Reservierung** für **Samstag**.
8. Das klingt toll. Viel Spaß!

✤ When talking about days and months in indirect speech, change "heute" (today) to "an diesem Tag" (on that day) and "dieser Monat" (this month) to "in diesem Monat" (in that month).

1. Good morning, colleague. What day is it today?
2. Today is **Monday**.
3. And what month is it?
4. It is **January**.
5. Thank you. I need to update my **calendar**.
6. No problem. Do you have any plans for the weekend?
7. Yes, I have a **reservation** for **Saturday**.
8. That sounds great. Have fun!

✤ In ancient Germany, the calendar was deeply intertwined with pagan rituals, marking time through the celebration of seasonal festivals that honored the natural world and its cycles.

1. Hallo Peter, wie geht es dir?
2. Hallo Anna, mein **Kopf** tut weh.
3. Hast du Fieber?
4. Nein, aber mein **Arm** und mein **Bein** tun auch weh.
5. Du solltest zum Arzt gehen.
6. Ja, und mein **Auge** ist auch rot.
7. Oh nein, und wie fühlt sich deine **Hand** an?
8. Meine **Hand** ist in Ordnung, aber mein **Fuß** tut weh.
9. Du solltest wirklich zum Arzt gehen, Peter.

✤ In German, free indirect speech blends the character's thoughts or speech into the narrator's voice without using quotation marks, often changing pronouns and tense to match the narrative flow, like thinking about feeling sick without saying "I feel sick."

1. Hello Peter, how are you?
2. Hello Anna, my **head** hurts.
3. Do you have a fever?
4. No, but my **arm** and my **leg** also hurt.
5. You should go to the doctor.
6. Yes, and my **eye** is also red.
7. Oh no, and how does your **hand** feel?
8. My **hand** is fine, but my **foot** hurts.
9. You should really go to the doctor, Peter.

✤ In Bavaria, Germany, finger wrestling, or "Fingerhakeln," is a traditional sport where two competitors try to pull each other across a table using only a leather band looped around their fingers.

1. Guten Morgen, **Lehrer**. Ich habe mein **Buch** und **Notizbuch** in meinem **Rucksack**.
2. Guten Morgen. Hast du auch einen **Kugelschreiber** und **Bleistift** dabei?
3. Ja, ich habe sie in meinem **Rucksack**.
4. Sehr gut. Wir haben heute eine **Prüfung** im **Klassenzimmer**.
5. Ich habe meine **Hausaufgaben** gemacht und für die **Prüfung** gelernt.
6. Das ist gut. Viel Erfolg bei der **Prüfung**.

✤ In German, the verb must agree in number and person with the subject of the sentence.

1. Good morning, **teacher**. I have my **book** and **notebook** in my **backpack**.
2. Good morning. Do you also have a **pen** and **pencil** with you?
3. Yes, I have them in my **backpack**.
4. Very good. We have a **test** in the **classroom** today.
5. I have done my **homework** and studied for the **test**.
6. That's good. Good luck on the **test**.

❖ Kant never left Königsberg but changed the world of philosophy from his desk.

1. Hallo Peter, hast du den **Schlüssel** für das **Schloss**?
2. Ja, ich habe ihn. Wir können die **Party** starten.
3. Super! Ich habe ein **Geschenk** für dich.
4. Oh, danke! Ich liebe **Feiern** mit guter **Musik** und **Tanz**.
5. Ja, es fühlt sich an wie ein **Festival** oder ein **Feiertag**.
6. Genau, es ist eine schöne **Tradition**.

✤ In German, the verb is always the second idea in a sentence, even if the first idea is a long phrase.

1. Hello Peter, do you have the **key** for the **lock**?
2. Yes, I have it. We can start the **party**.
3. Great! I have a **gift** for you.
4. Oh, thank you! I love **parties** with good **music** and **dance**.
5. Yes, it feels like a **festival** or a **holiday**.
6. Exactly, it's a beautiful **tradition**.

✤ In Germany, there's a museum dedicated entirely to currywurst, a beloved street food.

TAG NR. 100: HERZLICHEN GLÜCKWUNSCH ZUM ABSCHLUSS DES HANDBUCHS 🌱

1. Hallo **Freund**! Herzlichen Glückwunsch zum Abschluss des **Buchs**!
2. Danke, Anna! Ich habe es am **Computer** gelesen und viel gelernt.
3. Das ist toll! Möchtest du einen **Kaffee** oder ein **Wasser**?
4. Ein **Wasser** bitte. Und kannst du die **Musik** leiser machen?
5. Natürlich, ich mache das Fenster zu und die Musik leiser.
6. Danke. Ich habe mein **Auto** draußen geparkt. Hast du den **Schlüssel**?
7. Ja, hier ist der Schlüssel. Und hier ist ein kleines **Geschenk** für dich.
8. Oh, danke! Das ist sehr nett von dir.

✤ In German, every noun has a gender, and this determines the article: der (masculine), die (feminine), or das (neuter).

DAY 100: CONGRATULATIONS ON COMPLETING THE MANUAL 🌱

1. Hello **friend**! Congratulations on finishing the **book**!
2. Thank you, Anna! I read it on the **computer** and learned a lot.
3. That's great! Would you like a **coffee** or a **water**?
4. A **water**, please. And can you turn down the **music**?
5. Of course, I'll close the window and turn down the music.
6. Thank you. I parked my **car** outside. Do you have the **key**?
7. Yes, here is the key. And here's a little **gift** for you.
8. Oh, thank you! That's very kind of you.

❖ In Germany, achieving a doctorate is often celebrated with a custom called "Doktorhut," where graduates receive a personalized doctoral hat filled with candy and funny quotes.

CHALLENGE NO. 10

PREPARE AND GIVE AN ORAL PRESENTATION IN GERMAN ON A TOPIC YOU ARE PASSIONATE ABOUT AND RECORD YOURSELF.

"Durch das Erlernen neuer Sprachen tauchen wir in neue Welten ein."

"By learning new languages, we dive into new worlds."

CONGRATULATIONS AND NEXT STEPS

CONGRATULATIONS

Congratulations on completing the 100 days of learning German! Your determination and perseverance have led you to succeed in this linguistic adventure.

You are now immersed in German and have acquired a solid vocabulary base, enabling you to understand and communicate in most everyday situations. This is a remarkable achievement in such a short time!

Throughout the lessons, you have developed mental mechanisms that encourage spontaneous understanding and natural conversation in German.

Be proud of yourself. You have achieved a level of autonomy that fully opens up the doors to the language and culture of Germany.

The adventure continues! To maintain and refine your skills in German:

- Practice translating texts from English to German.

- Listen to our audios on shuffle to strengthen and refresh your vocabulary.
- Immerse yourself in the language: watch movies and listen to podcasts in German.
- If you're using Flashcards, continue their daily use.
- Communicate in German, with native speakers or via AI.

Congratulations again on this achievement! And see you soon in your continuous learning journey. Tschüss!

WHAT'S NEXT?

Your success is undeniable, and to maintain your skills, continuous practice is essential.

Here are some ideas to continue progressing:

1. Review the vocabulary from this manual with our Flashcards.
2. Elevate your skills to a new level by discovering our intermediate-level manual or by exploring other NaturaLingua resources.
3. Join our online community: share, learn, and inspire others. Your journey can enlighten new learners.
4. Watch our video training and discover the secrets to mastering a language in just 100 days.
5. Fully immerse yourself in the language to reach new heights.

6. If you're ready for a new challenge, why not start a new language with our "Learn a Language in 100 Days" collection?

Learning a language is an endless adventure. Whether you deepen your knowledge of this language or embark on a new linguistic journey, the voyage never ends.

Congratulations and good luck on your continued journey!

ADDITIONAL RESOURCES

DOWNLOAD THE RESOURCES ASSOCIATED WITH THIS MANUAL AND GREATLY ENHANCE YOUR CHANCES OF SUCCESS.

Scan this QR code to access them:

SCAN ME

👉 **https://www.natura-lingua.com/download**

• **Optimize your learning with audio:** To significantly improve your language skills, we strongly advise you to download the audio files accompanying this manual. This will enhance your listening comprehension and pronunciation.

• **Enhance your learning with flashcards:** Flashcards are excellent tools for vocabulary memorization. We highly encourage you to use them to maximize your results. Download our set of cards, specially designed for this manual.

• **Join our learning community:** If you're looking to connect with other language enthusiasts through "Natura Lingua", we invite you to join our online group. In this community, you'll have the opportunity to ask questions, find learning partners, and share your progress.

• **Explore more with other Natura Lingua manuals:** If you like this method, note that there are other similar manuals for different languages. Discover our complete collection of manuals to enrich your linguistic learning experience in a natural and progressive way.

We are here to support you in learning the target language. For optimal results, we highly recommend downloading the audio and using the flashcards. These additional resources are designed to further facilitate your journey.

Happy learning!

ABOUT THE AUTHOR

 François Trésorier is a passionate poly-glot and an expert in accelerated learn-ing. He has developed unique learning methods that have helped over 31,400 people in more than 94 countries quickly achieve their learning goals.

With more than 7 years of research, testing, and developing innovative approaches for rapid language learning, he created the Natura Lingua method. This intuitive and natural method, based on the latest findings in cognition, enables quick language results.

When he's not creating new language learning manuals or helping his community achieve language results, François is involved in humanitarian efforts in the south and east of Ukraine.

Discover how the Natura Lingua method can transform your language learning.

Visit our website www.natura-lingua.com and join our dynamic community of passionate learners.

SHARE YOUR EXPERIENCE

Help Us Revolutionize Language Learning

I hope you found this manual enriching and useful. Our goal is to democratize this innovative and natural approach to language learning, to help as many people as possible quickly and easily achieve their linguistic goals. Your support is crucial for us. If you enjoyed this manual, we would be deeply grateful if you could take a moment to leave a review on Amazon KDP. Your feedback is not only a source of encouragement for us but also helps other language learners discover this method. Thank you immensely for your contribution to our project and best wishes on your language learning journey!

BY THE SAME AUTHOR

FIND ALL OUR NATURALINGUA BOOKS ON OUR WEBSITE

SCAN ME

We regularly add new titles to our collection. Feel free to visit our website to discover the latest releases:

http://www.natura-lingua.com/

This list is not exhaustive:

- English in 100 Days
- Spanish in 100 Days
- German in 100 Days
- Italian in 100 Days
- Portuguese in 100 Days
- Dutch in 100 Days
- Arabic in 100 Days
- Russian in 100 Days
- Chinese in 100 Days
- Japanese in 100 Days
- Korean in 100 Days

ESSENTIAL GLOSSARY

INDISPENSABLE WORDS AND THEIR MEANINGS

Above - Über	Actor/Actress - Schauspieler	Afternoon - Nachmittag
Airplane - Flugzeug	Airport - Flughafen	Allergy - Allergie
Alone - Einsam	Ambulance - Krankenwagen	And - Und
And you? - Und du?	Angry - Wütend	Animal - Tier
Anxious - Ängstlich	Apartment - Wohnung	App - App
Appetizer - Sofa	Appetizer - Vorspeise	Application - App
April - April	Arm - Arm	Arrival - Ankunft
Assistant - Hilfe	ATM - Geldautomat	August - August
Aunt - Tante	Author - Autor	Autumn - Herbst
Back - Rücken	Backpack - Rucksack	Bad - Schlecht
Baked - Gebacken	Balcony - Balkon	Band - Band
Bank - Bank	Banknote - Rechnung	Bar - Bar
Basket - Korb	Bathroom - Badezimmer	Beach - Strand
Bed - Bett	Beef - Rindfleisch	Beer - Bier
Behind - Hinter	Beside - Neben	Between - Zwischen
Bicycle - Fahrrad	Big - Groß	Bike - Fahrrad
Bird - Vogel	Black - Schwarz	Blog - Blog
Blue - Blau	Boarding pass - Boardingkarte	Boat - Boot

Book - Buch	Boss - Chef	Brain - Gehirn
Bread - Brot	Brother - Bruder	Brown - Braun
Browser - Browser	Bus - Bus	Butter - Butter
Buy - Kaufen	Cake - Kuchen	Calendar - Kalender
Calm - Still	Camera - Kamera	Canyon - Schlucht
Car - Auto	Cart - Einkaufswagen	Cash - Bargeld
Cashier - Kassierer	Casual - Lässig	Cat - Katze
Cave - Höhle	Ceiling - Decke	Celebration - Feier
Centimeter - Zentimeter	Chair - Stuhl	Channel - Kanal
Cheap - Billig	Checkout - Kasse	Cheese - Käse
Chef - Koch	Chest - Brust	Chicken - Hähnchen
Chicken - Huhn	Children - Kinder	Chocolate - Schokolade
Chocolate : Chocolate - Schokolade	Cinema - Kino	Classroom - Klassenzimmer
Climate - Klima	Clinic - Klinik	Clock - Uhr
Close - Nahe	Clothes - Kleidung	Cloud - Wolke
Coffee - Kaffee	Coin - Münze	Cold - Kalt
Colleague - Kollege	Colleague - Kollege/Kollegin	Computer - Computer
Concert - Konzert	Conference - Konferenz	Confused - Verwirrt

Content - Inhalt	Continent - Kontinent	Cough - Husten
Courtyard - Hof	Cousin - Cousin	Cousin - Cousin/Cousine
Cow - Kuh	Credit card - Kreditkarte	Culture - Kultur
Currency - Währung	Dance - Tanz	Dance - Tanzen
Danger - Gefahr	Day - Tag	Deadline - Frist
Debit card - Debitkarte	December - Dezember	Delayed - Verspätet
Delighted - Erfreut	Dentist - Zahnarzt	Departure - Abfahrt
Desert - Wüste	Dessert - Nachspeise	Discount - Rabatt
Doctor - Arzt	Doctor - Arzt	Dog - Hund
Door - Tür	Down - Unten	Download - Download
Drawing - Zeichnung	Drink - Getränk	Drink - Trinken
Drizzle - Nieselregen	Dry - Trocken	Ear - Ohr
Earrings - Ohrringe	Earthquake - Erdbeben	Egg - Ei
Eight - Acht	Eighteen - Achtzehn	Eleven - Elf
Email - E-Mail	Embassy - Botschaft	Emergency - Notfall
Employee - Mitarbeiter	Evening - Abend	Exam - Prüfung
Exchange rate - Wechselkurs	Excited - Aufgeregt	Excuse me - Entschuldigung
Expensive - Teuer	Eye - Auge	Face - Gesicht

Family - Familie	Far - Weit	Fast - Schnell
Father - Vater	February - Februar	Festival - Festival
Fever - Fieber	Fiancé/Fiancée - Verlobter/Verlobte	Fiction - Fiktion
Fifteen - Fünfzehn	Finger - Finger	Fire - Feuer
Fire - Feuer	First aid - Erste Hilfe	Fish - Fisch
Fitting room - Umkleidekabine	Five - Fünf	Floor - Boden
Flower - Blume	Foot - Fuß	Forecast - Vorhersage
Forest - Wald	Fork - Gabel	Forty - Vierzig
Four - Vier	Fourteen - Vierzehn	Freezer - Gefrierschrank
Friday - Freitag	Fried - Gebraten	Friend - Freund/Freundin
Friend - Freund	Friends - Freunde	Fruit - Obst
Fruits - Obst	Full - Voll	Garage - Garage
Garden - Garten	Gate - Flugsteig	Gift - Geschenk
Goat - Ziege	Gold - Gold	Good - Gut
Good afternoon - Guten Nachmittag	Good evening - Guten Abend	Good night - Gute Nacht
Goodbye - Auf Wiedersehen	Granddaughter - Enkelin	Grandparents - Großeltern
Grandson - Enkel	Grass - Gras	Green - Grün
Grey - Grau	Grilled - Gegrillt	Grocery store - Lebensmittelgeschäft

Guide - Reiseführer	Hair - Haar	Hand - Hand
Happy - Glücklich	Happy - Zufrieden	Happy - Freudig
Hard - Hart	Hat - Hut	Have a good day - Schönen Tag noch
Head - Kopf	Headache - Kopfschmerzen	Heavy - Schwer
Height - Höhe	Hello - Hallo	Hello - Guten Morgen
Here - Hier	Hi - Hi	Hiking - Wandern
History - Geschichte	Holiday - Feiertag	Homework - Hausaufgaben
Horse - Pferd	Hospital - Krankenhaus	Hospital - Krankenhaus
Hot - Heiß	Hotel - Hotel	Hour - Stunde
House - Haus	How are you? - Wie geht es dir?	How much does it cost? - Wie viel kostet das?
How much? - Wie viele?	How old are you? - Wie alt bist du?	How? - Wie?
Humid - Feucht	Hurricane - Hurrikan	Husband - Ehemann
I am - Ich bin	I am [age] years old - Ich bin [Alter] Jahre alt	I am a [profession] - Ich bin ein(e) [Beruf]
I am fine - Mir geht's gut	I am from [city/country] - Ich komme aus [Stadt/Land]	I am going - Ich gehe
I buy - Ich kaufe	I can - Ich kann	I give - Ich gebe
I have - Ich habe	I know - Ich weiß	I like music and sports - Ich mag Musik und Sport
I live in [city/country] - Ich wohne in [Stadt/Land]	I love you - Ich liebe dich	I miss you - Ich vermisse dich
I need - Ich brauche	I understand - Ich verstehe	I watch - Ich schaue

I would like - Ich möchte	I'm joking - Ich mache nur Spaß	Ice cream - Eiscreme
Ice-cream : Ice Cream - Eiscreme	In - In	Inch - Zoll
Indigenous - Einheimischer	Injury - Verletzung	Inn - Gasthaus
Inside - Innen	Internet - Internet	Island - Insel
Jacket - Jacke	Jam - Marmelade	January - Januar
Jewelry - Schmuck	Job - Arbeit	Joyful - Fröhlich
Juice - Saft	Juice : Juice - Saft	July - Juli
June - Juni	Jungle - Dschungel	Key - Schlüssel
Kilogram - Kilogramm	Kitchen - Küche	Knee - Knie
Knife - Messer	Lake - See	Lamp - Lampe
Laptop - Laptop	Large - Groß	Lawyer - Anwalt
Leaf - Blatt	Left - Links	Leg - Bein
Length - Länge	Lesson - Unterrichtsstunde	Light - Leicht
Lightning - Blitz	Liquid - Flüssigkeit	Living room - Wohnzimmer
Lock - Schloss	Long - Lang	Look - Schauen
Loud - Laut	Low - Niedrig	Luggage - Gepäck
Main course - Hauptgericht	Man - Mann	Manager - Manager
Map - Karte	March - März	Market - Markt

May - Mai	Maybe - Vielleicht	Meat - Fleisch
Medicine - Medizin	Meeting - Besprechung	Menu - Speisekarte
Meter - Meter	Midnight - Mitternacht	Milk - Milch
Milk : Milk - Milch	Minute - Minute	Monday - Montag
Month - Monat	Morning - Morgen	Mother - Mutter
Mountain - Berg	Mouse - Maus	Mouth - Mund
Movie - Film	Museum - Museum	Music - Musik
My name is... - Mein Name ist...	Near - Nah	Neck - Hals
Necklace - Halskette	Neighbor - Nachbar/Nachbarin	Nephew - Neffe
Nervous - Nervös	New - Neu	News - Nachrichten
Nice to meet you! - Freut mich, dich kennenzulernen!	Niece - Nichte	Night - Nacht
Nine - Neun	Nineteen - Neunzehn	No - Nein
Non-fiction - Sachbuch	Noon - Mittag	Nose - Nase
Notebook - Notizbuch	Novel - Roman	November - November
Now - Jetzt	Ocean - Ozean	October - Oktober
Office - Büro	Okay - Ok (in Ordnung)	Old - Alt
On the left - Auf der linken Seite	On the right - Auf der rechten Seite	One - Eins
Online - Online	Orange - Orange	Oven - Ofen

Over there - Dort	Painting - Malerei	Pan - Pfanne
Parents - Eltern	Park - Park	Partner - Partner
Partner - Partner/Partnerin	Party - Party	Passport - Reisepass
Password - Passwort	Pasta - Nudeln	Pastry : Pastry - Gebäck
Pen - Stift	Pen - Kugelschreiber	Pencil - Bleistift
Pepper - Pfeffer	Pharmacy - Apotheke	Photography - Fotografie
Pie : Pie - Kuchen	Pig - Schwein	Pill - Pille
Pink - Rosa	Plane - Flugzeug	Plant - Pflanze
Plate - Teller	Play - Spielen	Play - Theaterstück
Please - Bitte	Poetry - Poesie	Police - Polizei
Police - Polizei	Pond - Teich	Pork - Schweinefleisch
Port - Hafen	Prescription - Rezept	Presentation - Präsentation
President - Präsident	Price - Preis	Printer - Drucker
Proud - Stolz	Radio - Radio	Railway station - Bahnhof
Rain - Regen	Rainbow - Regenbogen	Reading - Lesen
Receipt - Quittung	Red - Rot	Refrigerator - Kühlschrank
Refund - Rückerstattung	Relative - Verwandter/Verwandte	Relaxed - Entspannt
Remote control - Fernbedienung	Report - Bericht	Reservation - Reservierung

Restaurant - Restaurant	Rice - Reis	Right - Rechts
River - Fluss	Roasted - Geröstet	Roof - Dach
Room - Zimmer	Room - Schlafzimmer	Round - Rund
Sad - Traurig	Safe - Sicher	Salad - Salat
Sale - Verkauf	Sandwich - Sandwich	Saturday - Samstag
Saucepan - Topf	Scared - Ängstlich	Schedule - Zeitplan
School - Schule	Screen - Monitor	Sea - Meer
Second - Sekunde	See you later - Bis später	Sell - Verkaufen
September - September	Seven - Sieben	Seventeen - Siebzehn
Shape - Form	Sheep - Schaf	Ship - Schiff
Shirt - Hemd	Shoes - Schuhe	Shopping centre - Einkaufszentrum
Shopping mall - Einkaufszentrum	Shoulder - Schulter	Singer - Sänger
Singing - Singen	Sister - Schwester	Six - Sechs
Sixteen - Sechzehn	Size - Größe	Skiing - Skifahren
Skin - Haut	Skirt - Rock	Slow - Langsam
Small - Klein	Small - Kurz	Smartphone - Smartphone
Snowboarding - Snowboarden	Snowflake - Schneeflocke	Social media - Soziale Medien
Soda - Limonade	Soda : Soft Drink - Limonade	Soft - Weich

Song - Lied	Sorry - Es tut mir leid	Soup - Suppe
South - Auf	Spoon - Löffel	Spring - Frühling
Square - Quadratisch	Stairs - Treppe	Station - Bahnhof
Stop - Stoppen	Stop here - Hier anhalten	Store - Geschäft
Storm - Sturm	Straight ahead - Geradeaus	Stream - Bach
Stressed - Gestresst	Student - Student	Student - Schüler
Subject - Fach	Subway - U-Bahn	Suitcase - Koffer
Summer - Sommer	Sunday - Sonntag	Sunglasses - Sonnenbrille
Sunshine - Sonnenschein	Supermarket - Supermarkt	Swimming - Schwimmen
Table - Tisch	Tall - Hoch	Taxi - Taxi
Tea - Tee	Teacher - Lehrer	Telephone - Telefon
Television - Fernseher	Ten - Zehn	Terminal - Terminal
Thank you - Danke	thank you! - Danke!	That way - Dort drüben
The day after tomorrow - Übermorgen	Theater - Theater	There - Dort
Thirteen - Dreizehn	Thirty - Dreißig	Thirty-Eight - Achtunddreißig
Thirty-Five - Fünfunddreißig	Thirty-Four - Vierunddreißig	Thirty-Nine - Neununddreißig
Thirty-One - Einunddreißig	Thirty-Seven - Siebenunddreißig	Thirty-Six - Sechsunddreißig
Thirty-Three - Dreiunddreißig	Thirty-Two - Zweiunddreißig	This way - Hier drüben

Three - Drei	Thrilled - Erfreut	Thunder - Donner
Thursday - Donnerstag	Ticket - Fahrkarte	Ticket - Ticket
Time - Zeit	Toast - Toast	Toast : Toast - Toast
Toaster - Toaster	Today - Heute	Tomorrow - Morgen
Tooth - Zahn	Toothache - Zahnschmerzen	Tornado - Tornado
Tourist - Tourist	Tradition - Tradition	Train - Zug
Tram - Straßenbahn	Tree - Baum	Trolley - Wagen
Trousers - Hose	Truck - Lastwagen	Tuesday - Dienstag
Tuesday, - Dienstag	Turn - Abbiegen	Turn left - Links abbiegen
Turn right - Rechts abbiegen	Twelve - Zwölf	Twenty - Zwanzig
Twenty-Eight - Achtundzwanzig	Twenty-Five - Fünfundzwanzig	Twenty-Four - Vierundzwanzig
Twenty-Nine - Neunundzwanzig	Twenty-One - Einundzwanzig	Twenty-Seven - Siebenundzwanzig
Twenty-Six - Sechsundzwanzig	Twenty-Three - Dreiundzwanzig	Twenty-Two - Zweiundzwanzig
Two - Zwei	Uncle - Onkel	Under - Unter
University - Universität	Up - Oben	Upset - Verärgert
Username - Benutzername	Valley - Tal	Vegetables - Gemüse
Visa - Visum	Volcano - Vulkan	Waiter/Waitress - Kellner/Kellnerin
Wall - Wand	Warm - Warm	Water - Wasser

Water : Water - Wasser

Website - Webseite

Wednesday - Mittwoch

Week - Woche

Weekend - Wochenende

Weight - Gewicht

Wet - Nass

What day is it today? - Welcher Tag ist heute?

What do you do for a living? - Was machst du beruflich?

What do you like? - Was magst du?

What is your name? - Wie heißt du?

What time is it? - Wie spät ist es?

What? - Was?

When? - Wann?

Where are you from? - Woher kommst du?

Where do you live? - Wo wohnst du?

Where? - Wo?

Which one? - Welcher?

White - Weiß

Who? - Wer?

Why? - Warum?

Wi-Fi - WLAN

Wide - Groß

Width - Breite

Wife - Ehefrau

Window - Fenster

Wine - Wein

Wine : Wine - Wein

Winter - Winter

Woman - Frau

Worried - Besorgt

Year - Jahr

Yellow - Gelb

Yes - Ja

Yesterday - Gestern

You're welcome - Gern geschehen

Youth hostel - Herberge

Made in the USA
Las Vegas, NV
31 July 2024

93169475R00167